A Love Supreme

A Love Supreme

A History of Johannine Tradition

Allen Dwight Callahan

Fortress Press
Minneapolis
2005

A LOVE SUPREME
A History of Johannine Tradition

Cover art: Detail of Apostles from a Catalán Romanesque
altar frontal depicting the Ascension of Christ. Copyright
© Burstein Collection/CORBIS
Cover design: Brad Norr Design
Book design: Allan S Johnson, Phoenix Type, Inc.

All scripture quotations are the author's own translation
unless otherwise noted.

Scripture quotations from the New Revised Standard
Version of the Bible (NRSV) are copyright © 1989 by the
Division of Christian Education of the National Council
of the Churches of Christ in the United States of America
and are used by permission.

Library of Congress Cataloging-in-Publication Data

Callahan, Allen Dwight.
    A love supreme : a history of Johannine tradition /
Allen Dwight Callahan.
        p.   cm.
    Includes bibliographical references.
    ISBN 0-8006-3708-9 (alk. paper)
    1. Bible. N.T. John—Criticism, interpretation, etc.
2. Bible. N.T. Epistles of John—Criticism, interpretation,
etc.   I. Title.
    BS2601.C25   2005
    226.5'06—dc22

                                    2004024819

Manufactured in the U.S.A.
09 08 07 06 05   1 2 3 4 5 6 7 8 9 10

To my colleagues and students at
the Seminário Teológico Batista do Nordeste
in Bahia, Brazil.

Como professor entre vocês, ensinei pouco.
Como aluno entre vocês, aprendi muito.

Contents

Acknowledgments

I happily acknowledge here three colleagues to whom this work is intellectually indebted: Professors Elisabeth Schüssler Fiorenza, Obery M. Hendricks Jr., and Daniel Boyarin. Elisabeth Schüssler Fiorenza pointed out that women mark the important narrative moments of the Gospel of John, and I have followed the nodes of women's agency that Schüssler Fiorenza traced over two decades ago.[1] And in her essay on Johannine tradition,[2] Schüssler Fiorenza definitively determined what is and is not Johannine tradition and why, and I have identified the literary legacy of the Beloved Disciple and his Beloved Community guided by her arguments in that essay. In his doctoral dissertation, Obery Hendricks applied Frederick Jameson's concept of "root conflict" to the development of Johannine tradition.[3] In a field sometimes transfixed by questions of redaction and reconstruction, Hendricks' dissertation treated questions of ideology and interests, and in my own humble fashion I follow here the trail he blazed there. Finally, Daniel Boyarin's essay on the significance of the term *Ioudaioi* in the Gospel of John is a masterpiece, clarifying confused and confusing issues of group identity ancient and modern.[4] He rightly traces the conflict inscribed in the Gospel of John back to its roots in the Persian period, while delivering us—if we would be delivered—from anachronistically reading Rabbinic Judaism and early Christianity into the first half of the first century. I claim neither that all or any of these scholars would approve of the service into which I have pressed their ideas, nor that they would agree with the conclusions I have drawn from them. I insist, however, that their insights are foundational: any contemporary, critical construal of Johannine tradition must presuppose them. I have done so throughout this book.

I also happily acknowledge a brilliant constellation of conversation partners from whom I have greatly benefited. My colleagues and students at the Seminário Teológico Batista do Nordeste in Bahia, Brazil, to whom this volume is dedicated, have given me nothing less than a second home: words fail to express the depth of my appreciation. I learned much from Suzete Lima's monograph on the story of the Samaritan Woman as read in the context of Afro-Brazilian women's lives, and learned even more in my conversations with her about her work as an intellectual and as an activist. I am grateful for the opportunity to offer a Bible study treating contents of the third and fourth chapters of this book with members and friends of the First Baptist Church of Matanzas in Matanzas, Cuba. Professors Richard Horsley and Sze Kar Wan met with me monthly in the spring of 2004 to help me think through issues of empire and ethnicity late into the night as we sipped Chinese tea, munched treats, and shared happy moments of the life of the mind. I am thankful for the interest and earnest of the Harvard Divinity School students who took part in my New Testament doctoral seminar in the spring of 2000 and those who followed my lecture course in the fall of 2004—good sports all, who bore patiently with my intellectual improvisations. I am also thankful for the kind consideration of the Trial Balloon Society, a consortium of theological scholars in the Twin Cities that read an early draft chapter and engaged me in a stimulating conversation about its strengths and weaknesses. I am grateful to Cornerstone Christian Fellowship for devoting a Bible study session to a portion of an earlier draft of this work in the summer of 2004; the thoughtful comments of Fellowship members helped me to improve the style and substance of this work. Professors Calvin Roetzel and Krister Stendahl—both esteemed senior scholars whom I am honored to count as dear friends—read earlier drafts of the entire manuscript, by turns suffering and correcting many infelicities and doing so with generosity and wit. And I owe a special debt of love to Carole Hovey and Lyn Hovey for their kindness and encouragement in hosting in their home the sessions in which I first began to think aloud with them and other fellow travelers about the problem of love.

The reader may be assured that what follows is so much better because of the aforementioned people who have graced my work and my life, and I am thankful for all they have done. But for better or worse, what follows is what it is, such as it is, because of what I and I alone have done.

Prologue

The New Testament Epistles 1, 2, and 3 John and the Gospel of John are the literary footprints that mark the path of an ancient community. Across time and space, the writers of that community share vocabulary, stylistic features, and the preoccupation with an idiosyncratic notion of love that they called *agapē*—the greatest of all loves. The community defined this love as putting one's life at the disposal of those one loves (John 15:13). Indeed the community came into being in the love of its founder and early leaders, and in the love of its members for one another: it was a beloved community.

This transcendent love, the greatest of all loves, is, in the words of the great jazz saxophonist and popularly canonized mystic John Coltrane, "a love supreme." Coltrane is not, however, the Saint John with which this literature has been traditionally identified. Near the fragments of the Artemis temple in Ephesus is the hill Ayasoluk, the remains of a basilica erected by Justinian in honor of St. John the divine or *theologos*, of which Ayasoluk is the Turkish corruption. Origen calls the author of the Gospel of John *theologos* (GCS iv, pp. 483, 484, 485). The designation of Evangelist is subsequently applied to John the *theologos* who is the author of Revelation.[1] Thus the ninth-century manuscript P (025), in which the Catholic Epistles follow Acts and precede the Pauline Epistles, shares with a few other manuscripts the superscript of 1 John, "The first epistle of John the Evangelist, Theologian, and Apostle." This Byzantine tradition claims an identity for the writer of this text. First John, according to the ninth-century scribe, has an author.

But we do not encounter an author in the text of 1 John, properly speaking. A writer, but not an author. An author has a proper name: the name of the author "permits one to group together a certain number of texts, define them, differentiate them from and contrast them to others. In addition, it establishes a relationship among texts."[2] The author's name, then, "seems always to be present, marking off the edges of the text, revealing, or at least characterizing, its mode of being."[3] Arguments over the authorship of the Johannine epistles, arising as they did in the throes of the canonization of the New Testament, have sought, under the name John, to do precisely this: "To give a text an Author is to impose a limit on that text."[4] The partisans of what became the orthodox appropriation of tradition impressed these texts into the service of orthodoxy under the sign of John the author: "The author," asserts Foucault, "is the principle of thrift in the proliferation of meaning."[5]

Though an author has a proper name, the writers of the Beloved Community have no name. The designation "the Elder" is not a proper name. It is a title: the title of the writer. In 1 John the Elder does not identify himself. Introduction is no longer necessary, for his audience knows him all too well. The writer identifies neither himself nor his addressees. The "relationship among texts" that we now call the Johannine Epistles, texts with writers but without authors, is not and cannot be a property of "Johannine authorship." In the development of this tradition, we have to do with writers, not authors.

The first writer of the Beloved Community that we encounter is the Elder. The Elder wrote what we now call 3 John first, as an appeal to the letter's addressee Gaius, a member of the church commandeered by the Elder's nemesis, Diotrophes. In the second moment in the development of the tradition, the Elder then turns from the *ekklēsia*, from the church as such, toward groups where he has the promise of wielding influence. Second John is addressed to a woman, "the elect lady," who leads such a group, and to whom the Elder conveys the greetings of another woman and her conventiclers. In the third moment of the community's development, after the occasions of 3 and 2 John, the Elder writes the occasional discourses that are destined to become the raw material for 1 John 2–5. He thenceforth becomes the Writer of the Beloved Community. An anonymous editorial board of disciples—"elect ladies" and their followers—collected and synthesized these episodic, elliptical summaries of exhortation, ethics, and eschatology, for dissemination among the circles that had become the Elder's second spiritual home. These disciples compose 1 John 1, redolent with his themes and vocabulary, as a prologue for the Elder's writings.

These themes and vocabulary come to mark what we now call the Gospel of John, a narrative representation of Jesus—the archetypal life placed at the disposal of those he loved. One who claims to remain in solidarity with Jesus "ought to walk just as he walked" (2:6). The exhortation to walk as Jesus walked is a prelude to the narrative reflection on the words and deeds of Jesus that gives rise to the Gospel of John. Various New Testament formulas refer to the "life" (*psychē*, elsewhere translated "soul") that Jesus gives on behalf his followers. *Psychē* in these formulas is the Septuagint's gloss for the Hebrew *nefesh*: "He [i.e., Jesus] gave his life on our behalf" (1 John 3:16), anticipating the language of Jesus' description of selfless leadership in the discourse on the Good Shepherd (see 10:11, 15, 17-18) and the Farewell Discourses (see especially John 13:14 and 15:13). The insistence on life over death leads to reflection on the life of Jesus, concern for how he lived. The life is "in the blood," as Leviticus puts it. That life, the life of Jesus, was the "blood of Jesus" that cleansed other lives: it removed the effects of sin from them. There is no suggestion here that the blood is shed for the sake of the lives it cleanses, as though it were a cost for sin for which God demands payment. The ideation here presupposes the high premium that ancient Israelite tradition placed on blood, indeed the God of Israel's reverence for it: the quintessential innovation of Israelite cult in its ancient Near Eastern environment is that "Yahweh reveres and does not require blood."[6]

That archetypal life of love, as love itself, could be efficacious only when shared. Life in the Beloved Community is life together. The most egregious transgression against the community is the betrayal of desertion—of "going out." The Elder warned the Elect Lady and her charges of the "many frauds went out into the world," those who go out and do not "remain in the teaching of the Anointed One" (2 John 7-9). This desertion is echoed in the betrayal of Jesus. Those who "go out" rupture community. Judas is the arch-traitor who "went out" (John 13:30) into darkness. For those who go out, there is only darkness: thus the Gospel reports that when Judas deserts Jesus, "it was night" (13:30). Those who go out are those who walk in darkness.

But with this horror of rupture, the communal rupture of "those who went out from among us" (1 John 2:19), the Gospel of John represents Jesus as the hope of reconciliation. Those who wrote the Gospel of John saw in Jesus' activity a fulfillment of God's promise to gather together all the far-flung children of Israel. In the fullness of time the Israelite homeland will gather outcasts from the ends of the world: "Thus says the Lord God: I will take the people of Israel from the nations among which they have gone, and will gather them from every quarter, and bring them to their own land" (Ezek 37:21). And God would restore Israel's survivors. Jesus is the catalyst of this vision of restoration of Israel as the harbinger of mercy and faithfulness (John 1:17). A merciful, faithful God commenced Israel's history so long ago (Exod 34:6); mercy and faithfulness now embrace the alienated and rejected, even the members of the Israelite commonwealth rendered ritually impure by disease, disability, and death.

Jesus' personal encounters in the first half of the Gospel of John dramatize this grandiose vision of reconciliation. His conversation with the Samaritan woman at the well in chapter 4 shows that the vision includes the Samaritans and overcomes the antipathy of their Judean neighbors to the south. The hapless paralytic of chapter 5, the congenitally blind man of chapter 9, and the fatally ill Lazarus of chapter 11 are the signs that God's restoration of Israel embraces the lame, the blind, even the dead. This inclusive Israelite vision saw all those who belonged to the commonwealth of Israel as the children of God.

The violent end of Jesus' life dimmed that vision. Though the Gospel of John tells its own version of the violent end of that life—the suffering and death of Jesus—its idiosyncratic rendition of the Passion insists that it is the life of Jesus that makes the death of Jesus important. The Gospel of John uses the language of the paschal lamb and its equation with the beloved, first-born son to describe the sufferings of Jesus. The point of these allusions is Jesus' righteous innocence, not his sacrificial death. This language serves not as the terminology of divine sacrifice, but as the metaphor of righteous innocence. At the same time, Jesus is the anointed, the messiah and king of Israel: for this cause the crowds of Jerusalem pilgrims greet him with acclaim, for this cause the priestly authorities plot his downfall, and for this cause the Roman governor Pontius Pilate executes him on the cross.

Against all odds and all expectations, Jesus survives his execution. His appearances to his followers signify more than life after death. Jesus not only returns from the grave; he returns to those he loves. His resurrection is love after death.[7] That love, a Love Supreme, became the common confession and the common possession of the Beloved Community.

ONE

Root Conflict

3 John

He writes, "[From] the Elder" (3 John 1). "The Elder" does not further identify himself, and none of the subsequent efforts to adumbrate his historical identity
go beyond ingenuity. The Vulgate and the Latin Fathers translate *presbyteros* here
as *senior,* and this suggests to the eighth-century Venerable Bede the reference
to elders in 1 Peter 5:1. Bede understands this passage as a definition for the term:
presbyteroi are those who have been witnesses to Christ's passion.[1] For Bede, this
means that "elder" is really a gloss for apostle; this agrees with what Bede reports
as the ecclesiastical consensus of his time that John the Apostle had written the
Johannine Epistles.[2] But Bede must aver to ecclesiastical tradition to derive this
interpretation. The term *presbyteros* in our text is vague with an anonymity that
later church tradition would abhor as nature abhors a vacuum.

He writes "to the beloved Gaius, whom I truly love." Gaius is the sole audience of the letter, as the singular vocatives throughout attest. The Elder counts
Gaius among "my own children walking in the truth" (v. 3). This is a love letter
of sorts, replete with cognates of *agapē:* the verb "love" in v. 1, the noun
"beloved" in vv. 1, 2, 5, 11, and the noun "love" in v. 6. The Elder begins by celebrating Gaius's fidelity to the truth and his love, to which unnamed brothers
testify. The writer then proceeds to his motive for writing—to intercede on behalf of his agents, those very "brothers and the strangers who testify to your
love in the presence of the assembly" (vv. 5-6). It is these agents of the Elder

that Gaius does well "to send forth in a manner worthy of God" (v. 6). They have gone out "taking nothing from foreign sources" (v. 7): "foreign" here translates *ethnikon*, the substantivized adjective, not the noun *ethnos*, "nation." It suggests people or resources foreign to the community, resources beyond the pale of the commonwealth of Israel. These workers are dependent upon the generosity of those with whom and for whom they work, those of the assembly.

The majority of ancient manuscript witnesses read in v. 8: "We thus must tend to the needs of such people, that we may be fellow workers in the truth," or "that truly we may be fellow workers." To be "fellow workers in the truth," or "truly fellow workers," is, by definition, to lend material support to brothers laboring in the community. In this letter the assembly is the forum "for the brothers and the strangers who testify to your love," in which truth is arbitrated by practice. This rigorous arbitration of practice demands that true comrades "tend to the needs" of those engaged in the work: "We thus must tend to the needs of such people, that we may be fellow workers in the assembly" (v. 8). The work becomes shared work as the means of the workers become shared means.

But the assembly has become the sandbox of Diotrephes, who apparently refuses to share—at least on terms acceptable to the Elder. Herein is the source of conflict that has reduced the Elder to writing, for writing is tied inextricably with conflict. His exasperation is almost palpable: "I wrote something to the church, but Diotrephes, who craves prominence among them, does not welcome us" (v. 9). Diotrephes is effectively running a propaganda campaign against the Elder's allies, "prating at us with evil words, and, not satisfied with that, he does not welcome the brothers and hinders those who want to welcome them. He even throws them out of the assembly!" (v. 10). To welcome people in the assembly means to extend to them hospitality and succor, precisely those things that Diotrephes refuses the Elder's partisans.

The Elder, nevertheless, exercises extraordinary restraint. Clearly he has in mind the actions of Diotrephes when he writes, "The one who does what is good is from God. The one who does evil has not seen God" (v. 11). The two sentences are askew. The second sentence would better jibe with the first if the second read, "the one who does evil is from the devil," or at least, "the one who does evil is not from God." The Elder stops short of leveling a thorough condemnation of Diotrephes. He does not point to Diotrephes as a counter-example of charity, but merely exhorts Gaius to eschew evil by imitating "what is good" (v. 11). The presumption of Diotrephes is the presumption of a brother, a brother among as well as against brothers. The one who does evil does not know God, that is, he does not "get it" with respect to God. Diotrephes is not "from the evil one"; he is not evil. He just does not "get it."

But he is a brother nevertheless. The Elder's judicious avoidance of character assassination is itself a species of the brotherhood that the Elder himself propounds. Love does not stoop to character assassination, not even assassination of a character so flawed that we would kill it to put it out of our misery. In love the errant brother, in spite of himself, does not become a demon in the Elder's eyes. The Elder sees him for what he is—one who has not seen God.

The Elder here commends his envoy, Demetrius, to Gaius in glowing terms, but otherwise without introduction. No introduction is necessary: Demetrius is well known to all the principals, if otherwise unknown in the literary legacy of the Beloved Community. Everyone attests to Demetrius's sterling reputation, "even the assembly itself," the very assembly upon which the Elder cannot rely to assist Demetrius. Demetrius's welfare is now laid to Gaius's charge. The assembly is a witness to all that has transpired: the letter is an intervention in the life of the assembly, which is mentioned in this short letter no less than four times (vv. 6, 9, 10, and 12).

The Elder draws battle lines with the ink and stylus he loathes to use. "I had much to write to you, but I wish not to write to you with pen and ink. Rather, I hope to see you shortly, and we shall speak face to face" (vv. 13-14). This lack of confidence in writing is echoed in the early commentator and editor Papias, who writes that the voice of living witnesses to the words and deeds of Jesus and the apostles is preferred to written accounts. This reservation was strong among those most literate of religious intellectuals, the Rabbis. The mastery of the Law, the ultimate sacred writing, was realized and communicated through the real presence of the Rabbi. Both Palestinian and Babylonian Talmuds present the Rabbinic literary heritage as an exclusively oral tradition, an "Oral Torah," transmitted in a series of face-to-face encounters between rabbinic sages and their disciples beginning with Moses' instructions to his associates.[3]

The Mishnah and other instruction in Oral Torah "were learned in the course of face-to-face oral interchange involving the memorization, recitation, comparison, and critical analysis of memorized texts."[4] Written texts of rabbinic teachings, however, existed from a very early period,[5] and the Palestinian Talmud acknowledges the contemporary existence of notebooks, instructional graffiti,[6] even written forms of oral instruction delivered in the mail.[7] But the Talmud attests to Rabbinical ambivalence toward scribal recording of oral instruction. This ambivalence is illustrated in the Babylonian discussion of a report that the sage Rav Dimi wanted to send a letter to Rav Yosef bearing the correct wording of a Mishnaic passage: "Now even if he had found someone to write the letter, could he have sent it? For surely said R. Abba b. Hiyya b. Abba, said R. Yohanan: Those who write down legal traditions (halakhot) are like those who burn the Torah. And anyone who studies from them receives no reward."[8]

Like the Rabbinic sages of the Talmuds, the Elder prefers presence to paper: he prefers to speak, as the Greek here and in 2 John 12 literally translates the Hebrew idiom, *peh el-peh*, "mouth to mouth." The idiom is often rendered in English as "face to face," but this rendering will not do. The idioms with *peh*, 'mouth,' are to be contrasted to those with *penê*, "face" or "surface." In the Hebrew Bible people speak "face to face" (Deut 5:4), but there the encounter of faces is the encounter of surfaces, connoting opposition—a "face-off," so to speak. And so to be before or against someone in a posture of confrontation is to be *bifnê*, "in the face of" that person (Deut 21:16; Josh 10:8; 2 Sam 15:18). *Penê dabar*, literally "the face of a matter," is the appearance of a thing, its "face value."

But God speaks to Moses *peh el-peh*, "mouth to mouth" (Num 12:8). To speak "mouth to mouth" means to speak to another intimately, personally, tenderly. Tender and sensitive, the nerve-filled surface of the lips is unlike any other skin on the body: they are the anatomical marvel that makes possible the pleasure of a kiss. The communication the Elder awaits is intimate, personal, and tender. It is the kiss of kindred spirits.

The Elder closes the letter with "peace" (*eirēnē*), the translation of the Hebrew *shalom* that served as a general greeting and the opening and closing of letters in ancient Palestine. This distinctive salutation and the reference to the *ethnikoi* in v. 7 suggest the writer's Israelite heritage. The brothers with whom the Elder is in fellowship greet Gaius. But we must not assume, given the rhetorical situation of the letter, that Gaius is at liberty to greet all the brothers in the assembly. The problem addressed by the letter is that, in the clutches of Diotrephes, Gaius's assembly has repudiated the Elder and his agents. As the Elder himself complains, he must address Gaius because he cannot address the assembly at large. The Elder does not and cannot expect Gaius to be in a position to relay regards to "the brothers" of Gaius's assembly. Gaius himself may be in jeopardy; he may find himself among those whose hospitality has been hindered by the overbearing Diotrephes. If so, Gaius too is in danger of being expelled for being in solidarity with the Elder and his emissaries. Thus Gaius may relay the regards of the Elder only to his "friends." All in the assembly are sisters and brothers. But not all are friends.

The Elder seeks to recruit Gaius to be a comrade in his battle to do "what is good," to receive with love those who come in the name of love. He joins the battle with such grace that his careful words illumine the life of charity, communion, and care that he and his disciples after him would call *agapē*. In the next moment in the life of the Beloved Community, the Elder turns from the men of the assembly—Gaius, Demetrius, Diotrephes—to find kindred spirits among a few chosen women and their "children."

2 John

In the beginning, there was the conflict. In 3 John we find, in the words of literary critic Frederick Jameson, the "root conflict"[9] of the Beloved Community. The letter, in the words of Latin American journalist Eduardo Galeano, "springs from the wounded consciousness of the writer and is projected onto the world." The Elder appeals to Gaius to do what he can for his emissary Demetrius in the assembly commandeered by the Elder's nemesis, Diotrephes. We may assume that this appeal failed; the letter becomes "an act of solidarity," as Galeano puts it, "which does not always fulfill its destiny during the lifetime of its creator."[10] Gaius, Demetrius, and Diotrephes disappear forever from the tradition of the Community.

So too does the assembly. The word *ekklēsia*—usually translated "church" but which I have translated throughout as "assembly" so as to show that it signifies a gathering of people and not the building in which that gathering takes place— is used only here in the literature of the Beloved Community. After writing

3 John, the Elder then turns from the *ekklēsia*, from the assembly as such. But, the Elder's activity is not sectarian. He has not rejected the church: the church, by rejecting his emissaries, has rejected him.

Second John is an appeal to "the elect lady," a chosen authority in the community of the addressees: an alternative rendering of her title is "the chosen authority." The letter is also addressed to "her children," that is, all those under her authority. *Tekna* is the term the Elder uses to signify spiritual dependents. The interpretation of the addressee's designation as signifying a church rather than a female individual is an old one. Clement of Alexandria claims that this epistle is addressed to the holy church in Babylonia because he reads "to an elect lady," of v. 1 as a gloss for "the likewise elect [church] in Babylon" mentioned in 1 Peter 5:13.[11] The interpretation is as venerable as it is strained, and flies in the face of the plain sense of the text. The Byzantine commentator Oecumenius comes close to acknowledging the obvious: "He writes with commandments of the Gospel to a church or to some woman giving spiritual governance to her household. He writes this epistle to one of the women who have received the proclamation."[12] Apparently independently, this is the interpretation of the Order of the Eastern Star, an African American organization for the wives, widows, mothers, daughters, and sisters of the Prince Hall order of Masons. Eastern Star rites claim five biblical women as heroines: Jephtha's anonymous daughter to whom the Order has given the name Adah, Ruth, Esther, Martha, and Electa. "Electa" is the Elect Lady in 2 John. The sisters of the Eastern Star hold Electa to have been a martyr and assign to her the color red, symbolizing fervency and commitment.[13]

"I rejoiced exceedingly," writes the Elder, "because I found among your children those walking in truth, just as we received commandment from the father" (v. 4). According to the Elder, the truth is not something one knows; it is something one does. The truth is "among" the addressees insofar as they practice it, even though it is "with" them forever insofar as what is now the truth shall ever and always be so. The truth is with them, but not with them alone. The truth is not their property; they do not possess it. They are being exhorted to have the truth possess them. They are bound to the truth in their obedience to the "commandment" that they received from God and shared with the Elder "from the beginning"—the commandment to love one another (v. 5). This obedience defines love itself: "And this is love: that you should walk according to his commandments" (v. 5). This is what it means to "walk in truth" (v. 4); it is authentic love.

But authenticity is always attended by fraudulence. "For many frauds went out into the world," warns the Elder, "those who do not confess Jesus Christ coming in the flesh" (v. 7). The meaning of the present participle here, "coming" (*erchomenos*), is rooted in the Elder's theology of sanctified carnality. To "confess Jesus Christ coming in the flesh" is to testify to Jesus Christ in one's own flesh, that is, in one's own sanctified carnality. Confession is not what one says, but how one lives.

The Elder exhorts his addressees to boycott the inauthentic witnesses wielding influence in the community. "Every one who goes forth and does not remain in the teaching of the Anointed One does not understand [lit. "have," "get"] God. The one who remains in the teaching understands [lit. "has," "gets"] the Father and the Son. If someone comes to and does not bear this teaching, do not receive him into your home or even greet him. For the one who greets him shares in his evil deeds" (vv. 9-11). Fraudulence here is an "inside job." The content of the fraud is not the denial of incarnation. This is not a denial of the historical advent of Jesus the Messiah in first-century Palestine during the rule of Pontius Pilate. Thus there is no reference to these data, so important in the earliest Christian creeds. Also absent are verbs of denial and disavowal. The language here is strong, but the Elder does not charge the errant members of his community with denying the incarnation. Those misleading and those being misled have failed to affirm that the word of God has dwelt "among us." That affirmation is expressed as caring, concrete commitment: the solidarity that is love.

This is not a matter of creed, but of deed. Thus the reading of *didachē*, "teaching" or "doctrine" in v. 9 is especially infelicitous. We must follow the minuscules for the correct reading, which is *agapē*. *Didachē* is rare in the writings of the Beloved Community. The word appears only twice in the Gospel of John: a hostile context attends both occurrences. In John 7:16-17, Jesus responds to those who are amazed at his knowledge in spite of Jesus' apparent lack of erudition, saying that his "doctrine" (*didachē*) is divine in origin, and that those who desire to do the will of God recognize it as such. In John 18:19, the high priest interrogates Jesus about his disciples and his *didachē*. Thus the term is marginal in the traditional vocabulary of the Beloved Community, and ambivalent. Perhaps this ambivalence has its roots in the insistence of the Writer of 1 John that his "children" do not need anyone to teach (*didaskē*, 2:27) them. He is implicitly dismissive of *didachē*.

The ecclesiastical sensibility of ancient Christian scribes, however, placed a premium on doctrine, and its formation and promulgation were to become major projects of Christian theology. The ecclesiastical predilection for doctrine became the majority witness in the manuscript tradition. To read *didachē* as the more difficult reading (*lectio difficilior*), as New Testament text critics are wont to do, is to misunderstand, in the light of these developments, both *didachē* and *agapē*. In a choice between *didachē* and *agapē*, the latter is truly the more difficult reading. Love is ever more difficult than doctrine.

More than mere docetism is in view here: we find neither the verb *dokein*, "to appear," nor its cognates in the letters of the Beloved Community. The neglect of the sanctified carnality that the Elder advocates need be due neither to a Platonic abhorrence of the body nor to a Gnostic revulsion at material existence. It is neglect in violation of the commandment, thus the criminal negligence of one who, having carnal means, turns a blind eye and a deaf ear to his brother's carnal needs. Those being censured need not be Gnostics: perhaps they are merely fiscal conservatives. They are enemies of the Beloved Community, guilty of criminal neglect of the brother in need and so do not "bear this teaching" of sanctified carnality (see v. 10). Regarding such a person, the Elder demands, "do not receive him into your home or even greet him, for the one who greets him shares in his evil deeds" (vv. 10-11). To enter into cordial communication with such a person is to aid and abet criminal neglect, to become an accomplice. The Elder would not suffer Electa or her children to fraternize with the enemy of their common good.

The letter closes with an express ambivalence about writing that echoes the conclusion of 3 John: "I did not want to write with pen and ink, but I hope to be with you and speak to you face to face, that our joy might be full" (v. 12). The Elder desires to speak to his addressees "mouth to mouth." To write with pen and ink is no substitute for coming in the flesh. So in lieu of incarnation "many things" must be passed over in the silence that anticipates the fulfillment of presence. The Elder desires to come in the flesh himself. Only then may he speak intimately, personally, tenderly with the Elect Lady and her children. There are many things the Elder wants to say, and few he is willing to write. Even the salutation that the Elder conveys from "the children of your elect sister" (v. 13), another community under the authority of a leader whose position is presumably like that of the "elect lady," is so terse that several minuscule manuscripts and some manuscripts of the Vulgate fill it out with the phrase, "grace to you."

The Elder, of course, ultimately overcomes his reticence. For the Beloved Community—and for posterity—he becomes a writer. The words from his lips disappear forever, and only the words from his stylus remain.

TWO

Disciples of the Beloved Community

First John is not a pastoral letter, for it is not a letter at all in any formal sense. The features of an ancient Greek letter are missing in its opening lines. The first chapter of 1 John is the fruit of a writers' collective: the subject of the text is plural throughout. This writers' collective provides what is, in effect, an introduction to the single writer, the "I" of chapters 2–5: the Elder of 3 John and 2 John. Disciples of the Elder have brought together the Elder's discourses and they now disseminate them to shore up the embattled solidarity of the Beloved Community.

The writers stand in a different relation to the addressees of the discourses than that of the Elder. They are colleagues, brethren, and peers of those to whom they write. Thus they do not use the language of intimate authority that we encounter in chapters 2–5: chapter 1 contains no terms of endearment, no language of love in direct discourse. They speak of love but not to the "beloved." This explains the plural "we write" of 1:4 and the singular "I write" of 2:1, 7, 8, 12, 13 (2x), 14 (3x), 21, and 26 at the opening of the discourses and at the closing in 5:13.

The understanding that these writers who bear witness are eyewitnesses to Jesus of Nazareth is an interpretation that goes as far back as Clement of Alexandria.[1] "They saw the Lord himself present in the flesh," comments Augustine on v. 2, "and they heard the words from the mouth of the Lord that they have announced to us." But the writers attest to none of these patristic assertions. They tell us nothing "historical" about themselves or their addressees, and make no claims to authority human or divine. They tell us nothing of their background or biography: they do not even tell us their names.

The series of teachings that comprise 1 John is fragmentary. Direct address and axiomatic pronouncements introduce brief disquisitions. John Calvin called the style "abrupt and confusing."[2] "Teaching sparingly and exhorting variously," and treating nothing in an orderly sequence,[3] Calvin opined in the *argumentum* of his commentary, the text is reticent and elliptical. Its salient features are its polemical cast and the self-conscious use of writing as polemical discourse, the intimacy of writer and addressees, and a communal fund of experience that is the sinew of this intimacy. The rhetorical situation of this polemic is suggested in 2:26 and 3:7, which speak of those who, in the estimation of the writer, might and perhaps have already misled the addressees. The writer repudiates the errant influences on his audience by telling them, as he insists emphatically, what they already know, what they already have together and have experienced together.

Our writer writes of the experience he shares with his audience. At the same time, he is uneasy with reducing this experience to the written word. The reticence of 1 John signifies the writer's ambivalence about language and the ultimate inadequacy of words. Second John and 3 John respectively assert in the closing periods what 1 John implies through its fragmentary, gnomic style and lack of discernible genre. Our writer has judged words, words written (*logos*) and words spoken (*glossa*, 1 John 3:18), as insufficient media for love. His critique of the spoken word and the written word informs his discursive strategy. His language is allusive because words not only point to something else but also rely on something else, something beyond them, through which and by which language is made meaningful and in turn makes meaning. Only the face-to-face encounter compensates for the necessary inadequacy of words, especially the written word. True communication is communion, accomplished only in the encounter of persons, not the exchange of letters.

Nevertheless he writes. And they—the "we" of the prologue of this treatise—write. Their purpose in writing is different from the purpose of the Elder. The writer and the writers view writing differently. The latter have not written the treatise to inform the audience. Indeed they characterize the contents of the teaching as old news. They speak of what they and their audience already know, what they already have, what they already are. The affirmation of these things in written words—these things beyond words—is a joy for them: "And we write these things that your joy might be complete" (1 John 1:4). The writers have taken pen in hand for the sake of joy.

Prologue: Concerning the Word of Life (1:1-4)

In chapter 1 we have to do with writers. Credible testimony requires witnesses who agree. As we shall see in the next discourse, even as "I" write, "we" testify. And this testimony confirms the solidarity of all the principals with each other and with the Father and the Son. The first clause of verse 1:1, "What was from the beginning, what we have heard, what we have seen with our eyes, what we saw clearly and our hands touched," is the introduction by the writers, as opposed to the writer who writes in 2:1. It is the prologue for the clause immediately following, "concerning the word of life."

Verse 1 is a heading; an extended rubric that introduces what follows. Such extended titles introduce the expositions of the Elder, now strung together, concatenated like pearls on a necklace, in one text. The initial discourse opens situating its writers and addressees, both encompassed in the inclusive "we" of the discourse, in a present that is defined by the sensory traces of completed action in the past. Thus the perfect tense of the verbs signifies past action that was completed in the past and now constitutes the present. The central theme is the word of life, or the living word (adjectival genitive), or the word that is life (appositive genitive). This is neither the word of the Lord that we find in the Scriptures of Israel, nor the Word, absolute and unqualified, that we find in the prologue of the Gospel of John. The string of apposite relative clauses signifies what "we ourselves" have experienced together.

The temporal point of reference is to what was in the past, the reality of which still obtains in the present. First John 1:1, "from the beginning," is in the perfect tense, signifying the continuity of the present with respect to the past. The verbs of sensory experience in the perfect tense do not point to a preexistent principle before or beyond history. The phrase *ap' archēs*, "from the beginning," signifies that the word of life is coeval with the experience of the community, and that there was no point when the word of life was not audible, visible, tangible. This life was revealed, but the revelation is not, properly speaking, "apocalyptic." We have here not the verb *apocalyptein*, "to uncover," but *phanerein*, "to show," "to manifest," "to make manifest." *Apocalyptein* and its cognates signify the revelation of what has been concealed according to divine purpose. The sole use of the word in the Gospel of John, a quotation of Isaiah in John 12:38, is the exception that proves the rule that *apocalyptein* and its cognates are alien to the vocabulary of the Beloved Community. *Apocalyptein* speaks of uncovering that which God inscrutably has hidden from human apprehension. But the writers use *phanerein* to speak of the manifestation, that which makes itself available to human perception. "What was from the beginning, what we have heard, what we have seen with our eyes, what we saw clearly and our hands touched" (1:1): the inaudible, invisible, and intangible has become available as a manifestation that they could hear, see, and feel.

Greek mythology had bequeathed to Stoic philosophy a distinction between *zoē*, the life of the gods, and *bios*, the life of mortals. The Stoics further elaborated on the elements of human life, *bios,* as contemplative, practical, and rational.[4] But the highest aspiration of the Stoic was to live "life according to nature" (*zoē kata phusin*). In 1 John, the life (*zoē*) that is the common possession of the community is eternal (1:2; 3:14-15; 5:11-12). Incarnation is the direct experience, and so the testimony, of this anonymous consortium.

The emphasis here, as we have seen, is not on "the word," but on "the word of life." And the "life" is the life of the community. We may render the phrase in 1:3 as follows: "that you might have a common share with us." The word *koinōnia,* "common share," is usually translated "fellowship." But the word "fellowship" in English is too weak to carry the weight of *koinōnia* here. Because the issue of practical assistance to brethren in need is central to the ethics in the exhortations of the Elder, we must understand the fellowship referred to here as concrete, even economic.

Many have observed that literature of the Beloved Community neither speaks of the love of neighbor nor invokes the twin commandments to love God and neighbor that mark Jesus' discussions of the Law of Moses in Synoptic tradition. In the letters of the Beloved Community, the brother and not the neighbor is the proper object of love. But we may observe the literary trail of correlation of neighborly and brotherly love in the Qumran documents. That correlation is instructive because 1 John shares more affinities with the Qumran writings than any other New Testament literature.[5] The *Community Rule* enjoins a fulsome application of the command in Leviticus 19:18 to love one's neighbor. It says of the members of the community, "All will be in true unity, in good humility, with merciful love, and with righteous purposes, each one toward his neighbor" (1QS 2.24-25).[6] The members are "to practice truth, righteousness, justice, and merciful love, and to walk humbly, each one with his neighbor" (1QS 8.2-3).[7] As Boismard notes, here the Rule has appropriated the language of Micah 6:8 but in the concluding phrase, "walk humbly with your God," has replaced "God" with "neighbor." "Does not the alteration," writes Boismard, "result from the contention that love for God can be expressed only by love for one's neighbor?"[8] First John answers Boismard's rhetorical question in the affirmative in 1 John 3, where the Elder argues that one cannot love God whom one has not seen if one does not love the brother before one's eyes. This is, in Rabbinic parlance, an irrefutable *qol wa-ḥomer* argument: one cannot love whom one has not seen if one cannot love whom one has seen.[9]

In Qumran's *Damascus Document*, we encounter the interpretation of love for God as love for one's brother and concrete concern for his physical welfare. Each member of the community is commanded "to love his brother as himself and to care for the wretched, the poor, and the stranger and for each one to seek the well-being of his brother" (CD 6.20-21).[10] Here too the scriptural basis for the command has undergone modification. The model for the commandment here is Leviticus 19:18, "You shall love your neighbor as yourself." The neighbor of Leviticus has become the brother of the Damascus Document.

According to the theology of election, brotherhood sets the perimeter for covenantal relations. An Israelite is born into the community and inherits "all the privileges and responsibilities pertaining thereunto." The ancient Israelite heritage is passed on from generation to generation, from son of the covenant to son of the covenant. But a different principle guided the Qumranites as a community of goods. Brotherhood did not set the perimeter for covenantal relations. Covenantal relations set the perimeter for brotherhood. Membership was not a matter of inheritance. It was a matter of decision of members to submit to the rule of a common table and a common purse.

Community of goods was literally the law of Qumran. "And if the lot results in him joining the Community," stipulates 1 QSa 6.21-22, "they shall enter him in the Rule according to his rank among his brothers for the law, for the judgment, for purity and for the placing of his possessions in common." The word for community here and throughout the Qumran literature is *yaḥad*. The noun rarely appears in the Hebrew Bible (Deut 33:5; 1 Chr 12:18). But *yaḥad* is the term of choice in the Qumran documents for describing the association that bound the members to one another as "the community of God" (1QS 1.12; 2.22), "the community of the truth of God" (2.26; 3.6), or simply "the community" (1.1, 16; 3.12; 5.1; 8.1, 5).[11] The Greek translation of *yaḥad* is *koinōnia*, mentioned four times in the first seven verses of 1 John (1:3 bis, 6, 7) to signify both the relation the writers and addressees have with each other and with the Father and his Son.[12] The repeated reference to the *koinōnia* of the principals implies that the communal context of 1 John is that of a community of goods.

Philo similarly describes the Therapeutae, an ascetic community dwelling in the Egyptian desert in the first century of the Common Era, as having a community of goods. "There is no one who has a house so absolutely his own private property," he reports; ". . . there is one magazine among them all; their expenses are all in common, since they all eat in messes; for there is no other people among which you can find the common use of the same table more thoroughly established in fact than among this tribe."[13]

Among the communities of Qumran and the Egyptian Therapeutae, we may number the Essenes of whom Josephus writes (*War* 2.19) and the Pentecostal community of Jesus people in Jerusalem as Luke represents them (Acts 2: 42-47; 4:32-37; 5:1-11) as communistic societies in the first century of the Common Era, "groups whose style of communal life was a calculated rejection and replacement of the entrepreneurial greed of Roman commercialization."[14] According to all the reportage we have of them, all these groups were communal, requiring that their members surrender all their material wealth to a common fund. Some New Testament commentators have argued that the surrender of private property was not required in the Jerusalem Christian commune to satisfy the summary description of Acts 4:32: "Now the company of those who believed were of one heart and soul, and no one said that any of the things which he possessed was his own, but they had everything in common." The story of Ananias and Sapphira (Acts 5:1-11), however, a couple that surreptitiously refuses to liquidate all their assets and is struck dead by the Holy Spirit, is a serious sanction on any reading. We see similar rigor at Qumran. As the Community Rule says of its own stipulations, "such is the rule for the men of the community who agree . . . to separate themselves from the community of the men of perversion in order to form a community with respect to the Law and possessions" (1QS 5.1-2).[15]

The disciples of the Beloved Community likewise had resolved "to separate themselves from the community of the men of perversion in order to form a community with respect to the Law and possessions." The writers of 1 John 1 represent the teachings of the Elder in an effort to shore up their community against the appeal of less demanding alternatives to the common life. Apparently some members have already deserted the community of goods. The counterexample of the defectors was a threat to the unwavering, concrete commitment that the common life requires.

The Message

Talk about God is called theology, a term derived from the compound of two Greek words, *theos*, God, and *logos*, discourse. Theology is our discourse about God, "God talk," so to speak. The message (*angelia*) that the writers have heard and announce — that God is light and utterly devoid of any darkness — is the theology they share with their audience. As the writers of 1 John argue and the writer of 1 John 2–5 will argue, theology is as related to what one says about God as it is related to what one says about oneself. And what one says about oneself is validated or invalidated by what one does.

"And this is the message that we have heard from him and announce to you" (1:5): the phrase "from him" refers to the Elder. The proclamation of the writers is followed by conditional clauses that are ethical diagnostics for the writers and addressees together. This is in-group language, of, by, and for the Beloved Community. This inner circle is the concern of the writers. The conditional clauses comprise the in-group discourse: 1:6—"if we say...," 1:7—"if we walk...," 1:8—"if we say...," 1:9—"if we confess...," 1:10—"if we say..." Yet the grammar is replete with the indefinite subjects of substantivized masculine participles, "the one who," and the indefinite pronouns "whoever" and "whosoever." The indefinite pronouns require subjunctive clauses, that is, clauses of conditional action.

Verse 6 defines lying as not "making" the truth. To lie is not to do the truth, not to "make" the truth. The verb *poien* means "to do"; but the verb also means "to make." It is related to the Greek word from which we derive our English word "poet." The ancient Greeks understood the poet as a "maker," one who "makes" things in the world with words. The truth is not something one "tells." It is something one does, something one "makes." People, as moral agents, are poets of truth.

To lie is to speak with words that are inconsistent with deeds. One lies when what one says does not comport with what one does, when one's walk does not comport with one's talk. To walk so is to walk in darkness. And to walk in darkness is to forfeit the poetry of truth that is life in the light of God. One may speak lies, but truth is something that must be done. One lies whenever what one says about oneself is inconsistent with what one does. One lies whenever one's talk does not comport with one's walk. When one walks in darkness, one's life cannot be the poetry of truth that it can be only in the light of God.

Koinōnia is the link between 1:1-4, the solidarity sought and shared by the writers in the prologue, and the conditions of this solidarity in v. 6 and its practice in v. 7. The *koinōnia* is the economy of the Beloved Community. Elsewhere in the New Testament *koinōnia* signifies a Christian economy for Paul (Rom 15:26; 2 Cor 8:4; 9:13), Luke (Acts 2:42), and the writer of Hebrews (13:16). The writers acknowledge and advocate a community that is a community of goods. In the love that is *agapē*, to "have solidarity" (*echein koinōnian*) is related to what we do when we "have a living" (*echein bion*), that is, what we do with those things of which we all have need (*echein chreian*) to live.[16] The Elder argues that the tissue of fraternal relations is *bios*, the material means of living. *Echein* emphasizes the concreteness of this solidarity:[17] it is a solidarity constituted by things held in common, not merely beliefs held in common. This concrete solidarity is what binds writers and addressees to the Father and the Son—unity based on the material bonds of solidarity that constitutes *koinōnia*.

Christian ethicist Paul Ramsey explains, "Two main interpretations of the meaning of Christian love are contending for acceptance in present-day theological discussion. One is the view that the primary meaning of love is to be found in self-sacrifice.... the second interpretation of Christian love ... [is] that 'community,' or the highest and truest form of mutual love itself, is the basic notion of Christian ethics. In support of this viewpoint one might cite the notion of 'covenant-community' so fundamental in biblical ethics, and the New Testament *koinōnia* ... interpreted as 'the beloved community' in which God's will reigns."[18] Commentators have strained mightily to understand the letters and Gospel of the Beloved Community as expressions of the first interpretation. But they are quintessentially expressions of the second: the *koinōnia* is the matrix of love in the Beloved Community.

Here it is the administration of one's living, one's *bios*, that qualifies one's life, one's *zoē*, as *zoē aiōnios*, eternal life. The blood of Jesus signifies this life: "But if we walk in the light as he is in the light we are in solidarity with each other, and the blood of Jesus cleanses us of every sin" (1:7). Blood is the traditional Israelite synecdoche for life (Lev 17:11, 14). Here it is a cultic metaphor for the life poured out for the sake of others, and thus a reference to the life of Jesus that constitutes the life of the community. It is not a reference to the death of Jesus: nowhere does the Elder write of the cross or the Passion.

The writers of 1 John 1 raise the matter of sin in their discussion of conduct, that is, in the language of "walking," the Israelite root metaphor for covenantal behavior. The *koinōnia* in 1 John, as that at Qumran, insists that each of its members own a collective culpability. To have a share in the community requires sharing its faults and identifying with them. This would hardly have been attractive to those who saw that community or themselves as beyond the problem of sin, and who may have been insisting that they "have no sin." Those who "have no sin," those who are beyond sin, are beyond the need for communal review of conduct and communal discipline.

Confession of sins was de rigueur communal practice in ancient Israel (Lev 5:5; Num 5:7). Confession was acknowledgement of transgressions against covenantal law (Lev 26:40). The induction ceremony of new members into the community at Qumran requires this confession, and shows how confession is inextricably connected with the collective welfare of intentional community. "All who enter the covenant make their confession," the Community Rule enjoins, ". . . saying, 'We have sinned, we have been guilty, we and our fathers before us in walking contrary to the precepts of the truth'" (1QS 1.24-25).[19] Boismard has pointed out that the imperative of confession follows on the heels of the opening treatment of *koinōnia* in 1 John 1. As in the ancient Israelite tradition of convenantal community, life together in the Beloved Community requires confession of sin.

"If we say that we have no sin, we mislead ourselves, and the truth is not in us" (1:8). The trustworthy and just agent of v. 9 is God: "If we confess our sins, he is trustworthy and just so that he might release our sins from us and cleanse us of every injustice." The declaration of faithfulness and justice echoes the formula in Psalm 140 [141]:5 LXX, and later in *1 Clement* 27.1 and 60.1 (see also 56.5), a confession of God's fidelity to his promises and his commitment to justice.[20] God will surely forgive sin, and just as surely God will judge it. The writers remind their addressees of the divine certainty that sin confessed is sin forgiven, and sin denied is sin condemned. This double movement of forgiveness and cleansing, the arrest of sin's present influence and past effects, realigns words with deeds: "If we confess our sins, he is trustworthy and just so that he might release our sins from us and cleanse us of every injustice. If we say that we have not sinned, we make him a liar and his word is not in us" (1:9-10). By confessing one brings the anarchy of one's past actions under the government of truth. Through confession one returns to fidelity by telling the truth about one's very infidelity. One returns to justice by telling the truth about one's very injustice. And one returns to honesty by telling the truth about one's very falsehood. Without confession, the truth cannot be "with us."

"I Write These Things to You"

All that has gone before in chapter 1 is the prologue for chapters 2–5. The Elder begins with a statement of purpose: "My little children, I write these things to you that you might not sin" (2:1). The statement of purpose for writing is the Elder's way of introducing a discourse. He does this again at the end of the tractate: "I wrote these things to you all so that you might know that you are holding fast to eternal life, and so that you might trust in the name of the Son of God" (5:13). Whereas the writers speak of conditions, the writer asserts criteria that by their grammatical openness in principle extend his teaching beyond any one sect or circle. The phrases "whoever," "the one who," and "everyone who," have a universal reach. Conditions apply to "us." Criteria apply to all.

"This is reparation concerning our sins, not only for ours but also concerning the entire world" (2:2) does not refer to Jesus: the pronoun, "this" is masculine because the masculine noun "reparation," *hilasmos,* is in apposition. The pronoun points to what comes after, that is, the proposition that "if we obey his commandments, then we know in this way that we have known him" (v. 3a). Observance of his commandments is reparation for sin: only obedience to the commandments repairs the damage done by sin. This reparation is not a narrow, sectarian reality but a possibility for all humanity, "the whole world." The repa-

ration of sins and confirmation that one has known him is obedience to his commandments.

A New Commandment

The exhortation to "walk just as he walked" (2:6) and the Elder's claim that
he is "not writing a new commandment to you, but an ancient commandment
you used to have from the beginning" (2:7) suggests the warrant for knowing
what Jesus said and did. The ancient command to love takes on new life in the
life of Jesus: "Yet I am writing a new commandment to you. What is true for him
is so for us" (2:8). "Thus," writes Anders Nygren, "we meet again ... 'the old commandment which ye had from the beginning'; yet it is also 'a new commandment,' because it has received a new meaning through the love manifested in
the person and teaching of Christ."[21]

The neuter relative pronoun in 2:8, like the same neuter relative pronoun
of 1:1, points to what follows it in the discourse. The neuter pronoun "what,"
ho, anticipates the phrase "the darkness passes away and the true light already
shines." This is "what is true for him" and "for us." Verses 9-11 treat the imperative to love the brethren. Verse 11 conjoins an ontological description of the one
who hates his brother with an ethical one: he is in darkness and walks in darkness. The conjunction is epexegetical: to exist in darkness is to act in darkness.
One of the basic arguments of the writer is that ontology is ethics—being is
doing.

The Elder told his audiences before (v. 14) and he is now telling them
again (vv. 12-13) that their eternal life must not be wasted on affection for a
transitory world. The terms of direct address—*tekna*, "children," and *paidia*, and
teknia, "little children"—suggest that the addressees are under the authority of
those who affectionately nurture and admonish them. The Writer refers to his
addressees as *teknia*, "little children," throughout his discourses, literally from
beginning to end, in 2:1, 28; 3:18; 4:4; 5:21.[22] This is to be distinguished from
the language of father's son, *huios*, which emphasizes the activity of the son and
his identity with the agency of the father. In the language of the Beloved Community, *huios* is used only of Jesus.

The Elder's addressees are his children: but they do not belong to him.
Absent is any trace of possessive or proprietary language. He belongs to the
communities to which he writes. They do not belong to him. Nor is there any

assertion that the assembly has corporate authority, gifts, or grace. The Elder's rhetoric points to relationships with individuals, not institutions. These relationships are the site of incarnation.

Though the Elder addresses his audience as his "little children," he is not, properly speaking, their "father." He is, as his self-designation suggests, an elder brother. Likewise though the "elect lady" of 2 John has "children," she is not referred to as mother, and maternal language is entirely absent even as metaphor. There are fathers in the Beloved Community, but this designation is one of seniority, not authority. The Elder writes to "fathers" in 1 John 2 because of what they know and how long they have known it. They are responsible for the oversight of others by virtue of their experience of the word "from the beginning." Bede resists a narrow, literal reading: "He calls fathers not the aged but those who are older and mature with respect to wisdom."[23] I translate *hoti* throughout vv. 12-14 as "that," and not "because," because in each clause it introduces the content of what the Elder has written. These clauses are not arguments. They are affirmations. The Elder writes and has written to affirm his audiences in what they know, what they are, and what they have done.

The writer here addresses directly three constituencies among his audience: dependent children, men of age, and young men. The three groups are conventional divisions of a traditional society. The Roman moralist Plutarch has preserved for us a choral song sung at Spartan festivals: "Therefore in the Spartan choruses the old men sing: 'Time was when we were valiant youths'; the boys sing: 'so we shall be, and braver far.'"[24] Perhaps the gendered language here is instructive in the light of sociologist E. Franklin Frazier's comments about men and community stability, valid for any traditional society. Frazier observed that one of the reasons that American slavery was so destructive for African-American community was that a disproportionate number of slaves brought to the New World were adolescent males. Bereft of both guidance from an older generation and of responsibility for a younger generation, the adolescent slaves were crippled in their efforts to rebuild their damaged collective life. Their moorings to ancestry and progeny shattered, they were set adrift in anomie: "Young males, it will be readily agreed, are poor bearers of the cultural heritage of a people."[25] The Elder is concerned about this vital and fragile link in the community's intergenerational chain.

The discourse on darkness is linked to the discourse about the world in 2:15-17. The command, "Stop loving the world and the things of the world" (2:15), is not merely a prohibition but an order to cease and desist: some of the Elder's addressees are already enamored of the world that he deplores. "The world" here signifies the social and political system of society "in a pejorative and concrete sense."[26] In this sense the world, comments Clement of Alexandria, "is not the creation, but worldly human beings living according to lust."[27] The writer delineates the three features of the world of which his addressees must beware: "everything in the world—the lust of the flesh, the lust of the eyes, and the arrogance of living—is not from the Father, but from the world" (2:16). There is the appetite for those things we have, "the lust of the flesh." There is the desire for those things we do not have, "the lust of the eyes." And there is the pride of *bios*, of "making it," the acute satisfaction of appetite that feeds the chronic dissatisfaction of desire. The writer calls his audience from appetite, desire, and pride because they are all preoccupations with what is passing away. Those so driven are doomed to pass away like the vanity that drives them. But the will of God endures forever. So too those who do God's will.

Christ and Antichrists (2:18-27)

The Elder cautions, "Little children, these are hard times. And just as you have heard, an antichrist comes" (2:18). *Eschaton* may mean "extreme," "utmost," "worse," "meanest." The phrase is a *hapax legomenon* in the New Testament. It is anarthrous, thus the conventional translation "the last hour" is infelicitous; the phrase signifies not a specific eschatological moment but, generally speaking, "the worst of times." Had Dickens written A *Tale of Two Cities* in Koine, he would have used this phrase as the latter predicate in the first sentence of the novel. Eschatology here is not discourse on the end of the world. It is life *in extremis*, and it argues that life *in extremis* is not the end of the world.

The entire context here disavows typical apocalyptic expectations informed by 2 Thessalonians 2:1-2 and, erroneously, the Apocalypse, where the term "antichrist" does not appear. The antichrist of the Johannine epistles (1 John 2:18 [plural], 22; 4:3; 2 John 7) is not to be identified with any of the various apocalyptic false prophets of ancient Jewish and Christian eschatology. The false prophets of the Markan apocalypse (Mark 13:6, 22 and parallels), "the lawless one" (2 Thess 2:3-12), the second beast of the Apocalypse (Rev 12:18–13:10; 13:11-18), and the "deceiver of the world" (*kosmoplanos*) foretold in *Didache* 16.4 all perform miracles and are attended by supernal portents. None of them are referred to as "antichrist" in Israelite literature. Satan is first identified with the antichrist in the *Sibylline Oracles* (3.63-74) and thus no earlier than the end of the first century.[28]

"Antichrist" is also without a definite article, and necessarily so. There is not one but several antichrists who have come and gone. Here as in 2 John 7, the term antichrist does not signify a mythical, eschatological figure. The Elder defines his terms with polemic sharpness. What he means by antichrist is un-ambiguous: "Who is the liar, but he who denies that Jesus is the messiah? That one is the antichrist, the one who denies the father and the son" (2:22). Antichrists are not harbingers of the end of the age, but apostates whose advent charac-terizes contemporary times as "the worst of times." It is a moment marked by inauthenticity, apostasy, and pretension. "They came out from us but were not of us, for if they had been of us they would have remained with us" (2:19): those who are antichrists were once in fellowship with the community, but no longer. Because they did not remain with the community they prove themselves not to have belonged to the community. Those who are truly in solidarity remain so. The one who does the will of God remains forever in solidarity with the com-munity of sisters and brothers to which the writer belongs and to which he writes.

The prefix *anti* may signify hostility, "against." But it also has the sense of substitution or replacement, "instead of," "in place of." These other anointed ones understand themselves or are being understood as God's anointed instead of Jesus. They are usurpers of the unique status of the divinely anointed one. The treatment of messianism and unction here is bound together by the etymol-ogy of *christos*, "anointed one," translating *meshiaḥ* in the LXX.[29]

For the writer, there is only one, authentic, anointed one, and that is Jesus. Any other anointed ones are necessarily making a counter-claim to Jesus' exclu-sive anointing, and so denying the exclusivity of that anointing, that is, that Jesus is the Christ: not a christ, but the Christ. The metaphor of father and son here signifies this exclusivity and identifies the activity of the Jesus with the agency of God. God is "the holy one," a favorite epithet for God and an Israelite circumlocution for the divine name. At the same time the writer insists that those who have an anointing from God recognize that Jesus alone is the Anointed. The emphasis of the clause is on the definite article: the writer does not use definite articles when referring to antichrists. The counterfeit anointing of the antichrists is discerned by the genuine anointing, "an anointing from the Holy One," that is, from God. There is no authentic anointed one but Jesus. No one in the community, therefore, can legitimately claim to be an anointed one. All the addressees share a holy unction. It is a common possession. Those possessing a genuine anointing know the authenticity of the Anointed One, Jesus Christ, and the inauthentic anointing of other so-called anointed ones.

Just as writer and audience affirm the word that was from the beginning, they do so only by remaining in solidarity to the end. Their solidarity, realized in their refusal of the world and their refusal to desert each other, is the practice enjoined by the ancient proclamation, "what you have heard from the beginning" (2:24). Only if they hold fast to that proclamation shall they "remain with the father and the son" (2:24). The solidarity of antichrists is inauthentic because it is ephemeral. Those whom the Elder opposes had been partners to the *koinōnia*. Perhaps they claim to continue to be partners, though their deeds, according to the Elder, do not comport with that claim.[30]

The writer reaffirms the truth of the common experience of the community, and demands that those who have participated in that truth but who do not affirm it necessarily deny it. There is only confession or denial. And to deny is to lie, for to deny is to say "no" to the truth. "Everyone who denies the son does not understand the father. The one who confesses the son understands the father" (2:23). The verb here is *echein*, "to have," meaning "to know." Whoever rejects the son does not "have," does not "get it" with respect to the father.

Truth as Manifestation

These discourses of the Elder are marked by references to writing. The first discourse begins with the Elder writing to his "little children" in the present tense "concerning sins" and ends with the Elder writing to his "little children" that their sins have been forgiven (2:12). Likewise, the clause "I wrote" introduces the Elder's warning to the addressees to remain in what they have had from the beginning—"the word of God" (2:14), "what you heard from the beginning"

(2:24), "the anointing" (2:27). The phrase of 2:27b, "remain with him just as it has taught you," is transitional for the discourse of 2:28—3:12, which is held together by the phrase "remain in him."[31] The subject of the verb "taught" is grammatically ambiguous, but must be the Anointed One, Jesus. He has taught those who bear the anointing.

The writer asserts the divine paternity of the community: "Beloved, we are now the children of God" (3:2). The ancient Greek poet Cleanthes praises the god Zeus as the father of humanity, and Plato had described Zeus as the generative father of human beings (*ho gennesas pater, Timaeus* 37C). This language is echoed in Philo's discussion of God as the creator of humanity (*Opif.* 84). God is the "husband and father of the universe, supplying, as He does, the germs of life" (*Det.* 147; see *Som.* 2.273; *Mut.* 205).[32] But we do not find in 1 John an argument for the universal fatherhood of God that we encounter in the Stoa. The letter may be similar, but the spirit could not be more different. Divine paternity here is ethical. Adoptionist language in ancient Israelite tradition, historical when applied to Israel collectively (Deut 32:18) and political when applied to Israel's king (Psalm 2:7), develops a moral dimension in Wisdom of Solomon 2 and 1QSa 2.11-12 and 1QH 9.35-36. The righteous man of godly wisdom is the man of virtue who, according to Philo, "alone is born of God, for he has registered God as his father and become by adoption his only son" (*Sobr.* 56). Though God may be the father of all creation, only those who are virtuous are the children of God. Divine paternity in 1 John is not ontological, historical, or political. It is ethical.

Just as the writer assured his addressees that they have received an anointing from the Holy One, he insists that they have been born of God. In treating both the anointing and the divine paternity of his "children," he is emphatic: "even you" have the anointing (2:27), and "even we are" the children of God (3:1), "we are the children of God even now" (3:2). And even though what they will be is not yet manifest, what they are is beyond doubt.

But of course, the writer writes as he does precisely to dispel doubt, doubt sown by those who have misled his children (2:27). The writer therefore affirms his children by reminding them of what they have and what they are. Divine anointing and divine paternity belong to all the members of the community together. There is no special anointing for spiritual virtuosi. If all are the children of the Father, no one is more than a brother or a sister, and no one is less.

The writer does not claim to have a monopoly on the community's spiritual capital. He writes to demystify any such claims by commending practical criteria. These practical criteria are presented in each of the discourses to follow in a substantivized participial phrase "the one who" or "everyone" and a finite verb: these universal criteria establish divine anointing and divine paternity. Thus the pattern that marks the beginning of each discourse: the call with an endearing vocative, the command with an ethical imperative, and a criterion with universal application by which divine anointing and divine paternity are to be discerned. The universal criteria, however, are specifically addressed to the recipients.

The direct address evinces the relationship of authority ("little children," *teknia*) that the writer has with his original audiences. But along with this authority, integral to it, is the intimacy of the "beloved" (*agapētoi*). The writer begins and ends his discourses with these intimate vocatives (2:1, "my little children," *teknia mou*; 5:21, "little children," *teknia*). As we have seen, chapter 1 contains none of these intimate vocatives. The relation of the writers to their audience is the confraternal familiarity of "we" and "us."

"For we shall see him as he is. And everyone who harbors this hope exercises himself to be holy, just as he is holy" (3:2-3). Jesus was made manifest in the world to display his repudiation of transgressions: he "set sins aside." Sanctification, setting aside oneself to be holy, is the setting aside of sins, the repudiation of discrete, specific transgressions. Those who have the hope of seeing the son sanctify themselves; they exercise themselves to holiness, just as he is holy. The point here is to appear, to be made manifest in a way consistent with one's hope. This hope does not make one holy; sanctification is the evidence of one's hope. To hope is to make oneself holy. Hope too is a matter of ethics, a matter of action.

Love and Justice

The "message" that "God is light" is an ethical statement. The original message is one of justice: "Everyone who is not doing what is just, that is, not loving his brother, is not of God" (3:10). The writer has said all that has been said about what the addressees have heard "from the beginning" so that they "might love one another" (3:11).

The classical example of the failure of brotherly agape is taken from the Primeval History of Genesis, not the history of one nation but of all peoples, hearkening back to a time before nations, even before urban culture in which national identities define their distinctive arts and sciences. Reference here is to the Bible's first fratricide in Genesis 4. It is not the meritorious Abel but the murderous Cain that receives special attention: "Not as Cain of the evil one who even slew his brother. And why did he slay his brother? Because his own deeds were evil and his brother's just" (3:12). The word rendered as "slay" in 3: 12, *sphazein* has no connotation of sacrifice here: it emphasizes death brought about violently by the hand of another.[33] The problem of hatred, of violence and murder, is a problem of brothers. It is not a problem, properly speaking, of sisters. Violence in the world has always been primarily violence between men: it is the corruption of fraternity—not sorority—that results in bloodshed. After the advent of fratricide, even birth, the act of a woman bringing a man into the world, brings forth a life that but compensates for a violent death. "Adam lay with his wife again, and she gave birth to a son and named him Seth, saying, 'God has granted me another child in place of Abel, since Cain killed him," (Gen 4:25): Seth is not celebrated at birth for his own sake, but as a replacement for the fallen Abel. Murder takes life and diminishes the lives that survive it.

In the biblical account, Cain's sacrifice is rejected without explanation. Ancient exegetes moved to fill the narrative vacuum so suggestive of divine whimsy. *Midrash Tanḥuma* 9 explains, "'And Cain brought to the Lord an offering of the fruit of the ground' (Gen 4:3)—What does this imply? The ordinary fruit [rather than the first fruits reserved for God]." Philo explains Gen 4:3 with the following comment on Cain and his offering. "There are here two indictments of this self-lover [Cain]. One is that he made an offering to God 'after some days' and not right away; the other that it was 'of the fruit' but not of the first fruit" (*Sacr.* 52). That fruit, according to *Genesis Rabba* 22.5, was "from the leftovers." Ephraim the Syrian explains, "Abel chose and brought for sacrifice from the firstborn and the fattest, but Cain brought [merely] the fruits he found at the time. . . . [God] chose not to accept his sacrifice from him in order to teach him how it was to be offered up. For Cain had bulls and calves, nor did he lack other animals and fowl that he might sacrifice. But these he did not bring on the day of the first fruit offering, but brought the fruit of his land" (*Commentary on Genesis* 3.2).

These interpretations still beg the question of why did Cain not care to give the very best, or at least the very first, of what he had to give. Though the narrative in Genesis gives no hint of Cain's motive, Jewish and Christian commentators imputed that Cain was ultimately driven by greed. Philo interprets the name Cain as avarice (*Cher.* 52; *Sacr.* 2), and describes Cain as self-loving and self-seeking (*Sacr.* 3, 52): "For Abel, referring all things to God, is a God-loving creed; but Cain, referring all to himself—his name means 'acquisition'—is a self-loving creed" (*Det.*, 1.32). Josephus also knows this etymology: "Two male children were born to them; the first was called Cain, whose name may be translated 'Acquisition,' and the second is Abel, meaning 'Nothingness' (*Ant.* 1.54). Acquisition thus characterized Cain's form of life and mode of production: "Now the brothers enjoyed different pursuits. Abel, the younger one, was concerned with justice, and, believing that God was present in every action that he himself undertook, he made a practice of virtue: he was a shepherd. Cain, however, was altogether wicked, and on the lookout only for his own profit: he was the first person to think of plowing the earth" (*Ant.* 1.53). Cain was avaricious, and so avarice flawed his sacrifice. "Now he [i.e., Cain] killed his brother under these circumstances: They decided to offer sacrifices to God. Cain brought the produce of the tilled earth and plants, while Abel brought the milk and the firstborn of the flocks. This latter was the sacrifice that God preferred, who is paid homage by whatever grows on its own and in keeping with nature, but not by things brought forth by force and the scheming of greedy man" (*Ant.* 1.54).

The interpretation of Cain's sacrifice as being tainted by avarice is implied in the New Testament Epistle of Jude: "Woe to them! For they walk in the way of Cain, and abandon themselves for the sake of gain to Balaam's error, and perish in Korah's rebellion. These are blemishes on your love feasts, as they boldly carouse together, looking after themselves" (Jude 11-12). Cain, Balaam, and Korah were all associated with greed and envy. According to Philo (*Mos.* 1.266-68) and Josephus (*Ant.* 4.118), Balaam in Numbers 22–25 is motivated to prophesy against the Israelites by greed, and Ben Sirah accuses both Korah and Cain of envy (Sir 45:18). "But Cain took God's commandment [to avoid envy] heedlessly," writes Augustine, "indeed, as the sin of envy grew overpowering within him, he murdered his brother with malice aforethought" (*City of God,* 15.7).

The *Targum Neophyti* of Genesis 4:8 gives the most explicitly moral reading to the rejection of Cain's sacrifice. "[After the incident of the sacrifices]

Cain said to his brother Abel, 'Come, let us both go into the field.' And it came to pass that when the two had gone into the field Cain cried out to Abel, 'It is my view that the world was not created with divine love and is not arranged in keeping with people's good deeds, but justice is corrupted—for why else would your sacrifice have been accepted with favor and mine not?' Abel said to Cain: 'No, it is my view that the world was indeed created with divine love and is altogether arranged in keeping with people's good deeds. But it was because my deeds have been better than yours that my sacrifice was accepted with favor and your sacrifice was not.'" The ultimate source of enmity is Abel's deeds, which, the Targum explains, comport with "divine love."

The writer of 1 John holds the same valuation of deeds: "One who does what is just, just as he is just. The one who commits sin is of the devil, because the devil sins from the beginning" (3:8). Just as Cain's murderous actions made him a son of Satan, so the practice of justice makes all its practitioners the children of God. "Everyone who has been born of God does not sin because the seed of God remains in him. And so he cannot sin, because he has been born of God. By this the children of God and the children of the devil are manifest" (3:9-10). Cain's offering was rejected, and his murderous anger provoked, because his deeds were evil. The good deeds that constitute love culminate in life for oneself and one's brother. Evil deeds bear fruit, as all evil deeds must, in fratricide.

The hatred of fratricide is death: to remain in death (3:14b) is to remain in its power, the destructive power of taking the life of one's brother. He who hates his brother becomes his brother's death: according to a saying attributed to Rabbi Eliezar, "Whoever hates his neighbor belongs among the shedders of blood."[34] Jesus' teaching in the Gospel of Matthew intensifies this principle: rash insult is judged as manslaughter (Matt 5:21-22). To remain in death is not to die, for Cain the murderer was spared from becoming the victim of murder. To remain in death is to be a killer. "The one who does not love his brother remains in death. Everyone who hates his brother is a murderer, and you all know that no murderer has eternal life remaining with him" (3:14-15). The life of a killer is the practice of death. The only sure deliverance from death is the practice of love. "We know that we have passed over from death to life because we love the brothers" (3:14). One loves one's brother or one kills him. One may love one's brother or one may hate him, but to do the one is not to do the other.

Love and hatred are the only options, and they are mutually exclusive. This dualism is neither ontological nor anthropological. It is profoundly moral.

The Elder defines the practice of this love. "In this way we know love: he spent his life on our behalf. And so we ought to lay down our lives on behalf of our brothers" (3:16). This is an argument for *imitatio Christi*, and reflection on the life of Jesus on which any appeal to *imitatio Christi* depends. This appeal to the conduct of Jesus is suggested in 2:6 as the "ought" that constitutes Christian life. There is a reprise of this appeal in 4:2 with the insistence that Jesus has come in the flesh. The writer directs attention to how Jesus lived, not how he died; he nowhere mentions the cross or even the death of Jesus. The insistence on life over death—the freely offered life, not the martyr's death—leads to reflection on the life of Jesus. "He [*ekeinos*, i.e., Jesus] gave his life on our behalf" (1 John 3:16). And one who claims to remain in him "ought to walk just as he (*ekeinos*) walked" (2:6).

"Oh, children," the Elder exclaims, "we must love neither with reasoning nor with rhetoric, but with work and with truth" (3:18). Without work and truth, one defaults to hatred, to murder, to fratricide. "Reasoning," *logos*, is pejorative here because reason and language are pointless without work and truth. One must not love by reason or through language. Logos is not sufficient. There must be a *prologos*, something prior to logos. Thus 1 John begins by pointing to something that has come to pass prior to the discourse; 1 John begins with a prologue, something before the *logos*, that makes the *logos* make sense. Reason and language are ultimately derivative: they derive from love. And without love, reason has nothing to think and language has nothing to say.

Words, spoken and written, are inadequate without work and truth. Our writer knows this, and this insight has constrained him to be a man of few words. This terseness has resulted in a style that says little because so much cannot be said, and repeats words because few words really mean anything. Without the vital correlatives of work and truth, speech and writing must be prohibited. Our writer speaks only long enough to tell his audience to stop talking.[35] "There are indeed things that cannot be put into words," muses philosopher Ludwig Wittgenstein. "*They make themselves manifest. They are what is mystical.*"[36] We cannot speak about them, and "what we cannot speak about we must pass over in silence."[37] "What shows itself is prior to speech and language and the basis for speech and language," historian of religion Charles Long writes explaining Witt-genstein's aphorism, "What can be shown cannot be said";[38] "furthermore," comments Long, "because it shows itself, it cannot be said—it is silent."[39]

The Elder insists here, however, that there is something other than language and silence. There is action. There is the act: by this gloss of the Greek *logos*, Goethe's Dr. Faustus solves his problem of translating the first verse of the Gospel of John. In the beginning, he exults, was the act. There is, Charles Long explains, "a mode of being that does not make itself known through the demonstrations of a language that stands for objects but through that kind of showing in silence which is necessary for speech and all the objects to which speech refers."[40]

The Elder must speak with his addressees face to face, "mouth to mouth," to fulfill their joy. He insists on a carnal presence that the Hebrew idiom conveys so compellingly—communication of the message at close quarters with the intimacy of a kiss. Yet the authors who edited into existence 1 John close their preamble by citing joy as the object of their labors. They are writing "these things"—transcripts of the Elder's discourses on transcendent immanence—so that their joy might be fulfilled (1:4). Though the Elder may not have agreed with his editors that joy could indeed be fulfilled with a stroke of the pen, as it were, both agree that neither the written word (*logos*) nor the spoken word (*glossa*) are sufficient for loving.

The love enjoined here is a love of the brethren. Herein we encounter what Anders Nygren called the "curious doubleness" of agape in the letters and Gospel of John. "The Johannine spiritual fellowship and unity is only possible as between 'the brethren,' whose unity is in God. But . . . love for man now becomes particularistic; it loses something of its original all-embracing scope."[41] But the argument of the writer is not that love is denied outside the embrace of the community. His argument is more radical: love is impossible outside the embrace of the community, for love is that embrace.

The *agapē* of the Beloved Community does not conceive of "man" [sic] as the object of love. Because God is love, love is something one neither possesses nor dispenses, for, like God, it can neither be possessed nor dispensed. Love is that in which one participates, as lover and beloved: the two, according to the writer, cannot and must not be mutually exclusive—his argument is that to be

one or the other one must be both. Love is not something that one has for another; *agapē* is what "we" have "among us," it is what we share with God and
with each other. Here Nygren gets it: "There is no specification of the object of
Agape; for as God is Agape, so Agape as such and in its own nature is a partici-
pation in the life of God."[42] The writer does not write merely of the love of
someone or love for someone. His topic is far more expansive and inclusive. He
writes of love as the predicate of God.

We cannot understand the "exclusionary" language of love here and
throughout the letters and discourses of the Elder without looking to the ancient Israelite tradition of covenant that constitutes the theory and practice of
agapē in the Beloved Community. For ancient Israel, history begins with love.
God liberates because he loves. His love makes him make promises, make war,
and make a way out of no way for those with no way out. The book of Deuteronomy fulsomely sets out the terms and conditions for the relationship of love
between God and Israel. Deuteronomy, "the biblical document par excellence of
agape,"[43] delineates "Yahweh's love for Israel, and the imperative of Israel's love
for Yahweh in return."[44] The most important word for love here is *'ahavah*. This
word and its cognates appear frequently in Hebrew expressions of conjugal love,
though Deuteronomy eschews the imagery of marriage utilized in Isaiah and
dramatized in Hosea.[45] Moran characterizes *'ahavah* in Deuteronomy as "a love
that can be commanded." "Above all, it is a love which must be expressed in
loyalty, in service, and in unqualified obedience to the demands of the Law."[46]
"If Deuteronomy is the biblical document par excellence of love, it is also the
biblical document par excellence of covenant."[47] Just as the Hebrew *yaḥad*
defines *koinōnia*, so the Hebrew *'ahavah* defines *agapē* in the vocabulary of the
Beloved Community, and both are principal elements of the ancient Israelite
tradition of divine covenant.

This accounts for why love relationships that Greek expresses with words
other than *agapē* are in absence in Deuteronomy's treatment of *'ahavah*. Though
the book treats relations between parents and children, it does not use *'ahavah* to
do so, and Deuteronomy makes no reference to marital relations. The intimate
relationship that is treated, however, is that of brothers. It is in the language of
fraternal relations that love enters the vocabulary of international diplomacy in
the Amarna period. In the correspondence between Tusratta of Mitanni and the

Egyptian court it is the principal topic, and denotes the friendship between rulers, who are independent and equals, "brothers."[48] In Deuteronomy, as in the suzerainty treaties that inform its language, "brothers" are the principals in a love relationship between equals, and covenant is the background of this apparently endearing designation. It is with this background in view that we must read 1 John's preoccupation with the material expression of compassion, care, and concern among members of the Beloved Community.

"But how does the love of God remain with someone," the Elder asks, "who has made it in the world and sees his brother in need and closes his heart to him?" (3:17). The word "heart" here is a delicate rendering of the Greek *ta splangchna,* literally, "guts, entrails," which the ancients understood as the seat of compassion. The Elder argues that compassion is not merely an emotional response, grief elicited by someone else's grief. It is material relief, the concrete expression of mercy. *Ta splangchna* is the ancient Greek anatomical metaphor for pity with a pocketbook. This is not the language of philanthropy. It is the language of obligation. The Elder asserts that compassion is a debt one owes to one's brother: "we owe *(opheilomen)* love to the brethren." To run away from that obligation is not a failure of compassion, but, truer to the Greek metaphor, a failure of guts *(ta splangchna).* To do so knowingly is to commit fratricide, murder in the first degree. As Latin American philosopher Enrique Dussel has insisted, "There are those who hold that morality and ethics are essentially ideological.... This is a false position. Morality and ethics are both corporeal, carnal, fleshly. They are infrastructural elements (understanding by this term anything of an economic or productive nature, anything connected with life and corporeality).... Our entire reflection here must remain on the level of corporeal, material, bodily radicality, which is consonant with the greatest holiness, if by holiness we understand ethical perfection."[49]

Spicq reads 1 John 3:17, the clearest statement of this preoccupation, citing "all commentators" who say that the verse "proposes so banal an exercise as material assistance."[50] Spicq here follows the classic lead of Augustine, who comments, "Behold whence love begins.... If then you cannot give what is superfluous to your brother, can you lay down your life for him?"[51] This line of interpretation suggests how far Augustine was removed from the material understanding of *agapē* in evidence elsewhere even in patristic literature. Canon XI of the fourth-century Synod of Gangra commands, "If anyone shall despise those who out of faith make love-feasts (*agapai*) and invite the brethren in honor of the Lord, and is not willing to accept these invitations because he despises what is done, let him be anathema."[52] In chapter 40 of the fifth-century *Apocalypse of Paul*, the Apostle Paul inquires about those in hell wrapped in blazing, sulphurous rags and tortured by dragons and angels. His *angelus interpres* explains, "They are those who seemed to renounce the world by wearing our raiment, but the tribulations of the world made them miserable so that they did not arrange a single love feast [lit. 'they did not arrange any *agapē*'] and had no compassion on the widows and orphans. They did not take in the stranger and the pilgrim nor present a gift (oblation) nor show mercy to their neighbor."

The writer's argument is that "superfluities" are the tissue of love, the stuff love is made of. Love is not expressed in material necessities: it consists in them. "The entire Christian economy is thus centered on charity: in the context of the Church—for it always worked out through loving one's brothers—to live is to love."[53] "This could be translated," writes Spiq in a summary gloss of 1 John 4:10-12, "'Behold, such is the economy of love.'"[54] In the Beloved Community, wealth in the world's goods is the only sacrament. Taken, broken, and shared, it is the stuff of communion.

The writer stands in the ancient Israelite tradition of social welfare at least as old as the various devices of distributive justice in Deuteronomy aimed at abolishing indigence in Israel (see Deut 15:4). A portion of the tithe and gleanings of every harvest were freely given to those without means (24:19-29). Interest was proscribed (23:19). All debts were to be cancelled (15:2) and slaves released from bondage (15:12-15). This communistic ideal informed the beatific vision of classical Israelite prophecy.[55] At Qumran, where, as we have seen, the spirit of Deuteronomy was everywhere in evidence, two days' worth of earnings were set aside every month to support "the poor and the needy, the aged sick and the homeless, the captive taken by a foreign people, the virgin who has no near kin, and the ma[id] for whom no one cares" (CD 14.13-16a).

The ancient Israelite tradition of distributive justice profoundly influenced Christian moral exhortation (James 2:15-16; Matt 25:31-46; *Didache* 13.3-7, which instructs the tithe to be used for the relief of the poor). Paul's collection was for the relief of the poor (Rom 15:25-28). The Christian commune in Jerusalem collectivized all wealth to provide for the needs of everyone in the community (Acts 2:42-47; 4:32-37), and faced schism over inadequate administration of the dole to widows (Acts 6:1-6)—the only biblical incident of grumbling that does not provoke divine censure. The Beloved Community remembers Jesus and his followers living out of the same common fund, which could be used for relief of the poor (John 12:6). An organized collection for relief of the indigent is a feature of Christian economic life well after the apostolic period. Ignatius complained that this common fund was being used to finance the manumission of slaves (*Eph.* 4.3). Justin Martyr attests to such a collection (1 *Apol.* 14.2), which he recognized as a concrete expression of solidarity among the churches (1 *Apol.* 67.6). At least as important as the *depositum fidei*, the traditions of faith and practice he called "the deposit of faith," Tertullian would later call this common fund the *depositum pietatis*, "the deposit of piety."

For John Chrysostom, 1 John 3:17 is an opportunity to exhort his wealthy audience to identify with the plight of the indigent. In passing, he also suggests the customary response of those in his congregation to their direct contact with the poor. "When you see a poor person, don't run away but immediately recognize that, whoever you may be, you are that person. What would you want everyone to do to you?"[56] The preacher invokes the logic of empathy here, and stops short of explicitly commanding compassion. His exhortation is a remarkable contrast to the text upon which he comments. Chrysostom's appeal to his hearers is a plea for empathy. But nowhere in the discourses of the Elder is there an ethic of empathy. Nor is there basis for a philanthropy that could direct the response of wealthy Christians to the poor they ran into—or ran from. This relationship forecloses the arbitrariness and volition that attends philanthropy—the act of voluntarily disposing a portion of one's material goods to another who has no claim on them. As Reinhold Niebuhr once observed, philanthropy "always compounds the display of power with the expression of pity. Sometimes it is even used as a conscious effort to evade the requirements of justice."[57] But it is precisely justice that the Elder demands.

The concrete expression of compassion, and so God's acknowledgement of it, is greater than the subjective sensibilities of the heart. "So by this we shall know that we belong to the truth. And in his presence we shall convince our heart. For if our heart condemn anything, God is greater than our heart and knows all things" (3:19-20). Even our conscience is not sufficient to judge our love. The heart is the seat of emotion, courage, the organ of affect. But it is an unreliable compass for the moral life. The heart is the place of anxiety. According to the Elder, the heart is also the seat of condemnation: "Beloved, if our heart does not condemn us, we have confidence toward God" (3:21). The heart must not be the final judge of truth. It is truth that judges the heart.

Obedience to the commandment is the basis for confidence before God. It assures that the heart's desire and the will of God are one. "And if we ask for something we receive it from him, because we obey his commandments and do things that are pleasing in his sight" (3:22). Elsewhere in the tractate the Elder repeats this principle of confident petition: "And this is the confidence that we have toward him: he heeds us whenever we request anything according to his will. If we know that he heeds us whenever we make a request, then we know that we have what we have requested" (1 John 5:14-15).

This commandment is the signal principle to which the text calls attention by the use of the formula *kai aute estin,* "and this is" (1:5; 3:11; 3:23; 5:14; 5:14). "And this is his commandment: that you trust in the name of his son Jesus Christ and love each other, just as he has commanded you" (3:23). The "and" that conjoins the two subjunctive clauses is epexegetical; the second clause defines the first. To have faith in the name of God's son Jesus is to love one another. The epexegesis of faith is love.

The Spirits

The spirit is mentioned neither in 2 nor in 3 John. In 1 John, however, the writer mentions the Spirit twelve times. The Elder exhorts his audience to "discern the spirits": "Beloved, do not trust every spirit, but discern the spirits if they are of God" (4:1). Johannine spirituality demands critical consciousness. And just as the addressees are confronted with inauthentic messiahs, so too they are confronted with inauthentic spirits: indeed the inauthentic spirit is defined here as antichrist presently at large in the world (4:3). These are Jesus-destroying spirits; Greek and Latin variants read here, "every spirit that destroys Jesus."[58] First John 4:2-3 is a dual criterion to guide discernment of the authentic spirit, the spirit of God: "In this way we know the spirit of God: every spirit that confesses that the Jesus Christ who came in the flesh is of God. And every spirit that does not confess Jesus is not from God."

In the confession of 1 John 4:2-3, as we saw in 2 John, to "confess Jesus Christ in the flesh" is to bear witness to Jesus in one's own flesh, in one's own sanctified carnality. Oecumenius comments, "confessing Jesus Christ having come in the flesh is to confess not only his having come in his own flesh but also in mine."[59] First John 4:4 introduces a disquisition on the adversarial relation of God and the world.[60] "The one who knows God listens to us. The one who is not from God does not listen to us. From this we know the spirit of truth and the spirit of error" (4:6). This criterion hearkens back to the root conflict in 3 John. Diotrephes refused to listen to the Elder and his emissaries.

Love and Authenticity

The practice that love demands, "let us love each other" (4:7), is the strongly stated desideratum in 4:11, "if God so loved us, then we ought to love each other." The tension between these two verses is borne of the hiatus between the "is" and the "ought" of *agapē*. Love is owed; to be beloved is to be indebted. And indebtedness introduces the possibility of failure to pay—the ominous prospect of default.

The writer points back to love that is not contingent in that it is already accomplished, already perfect, and so he writes of it in the perfect tense. God has sent (*apestalken*) his son. This verb, here in the fait accompli of the perfect tense, emphasizes the authority of the sender and the agency of the sender realized through the one sent: it signifies the act of sending by pointing back to the sender. The writer teaches that his children must love because they have been loved. "In this there is love: not that we loved God, but that he loved us and sent his son as reparation for our sins" (4:10). They must love because of God's preemptive love, which undoes the damage of sin. In 4:11, the writer refers to his addressees as beloved, *agapētoi*, one last time, warning them that injustice is sin that kills.[61] The Elder does not speak of intercession on behalf of such sinners. They are beyond intercession by dint of their murderous sin, the sin of Cain.

"God is love" (4:8, 16). In this repeated predication, writes Nygren, "John gives us the phrase in which the formulation of the idea of Agape reaches finality."[62] The Writer's argument is that agape is concretely defined, grounded in what we have seen. None have seen God: only those acting in love make God visible, audible, tangible. Later in the narrative form of the tradition we see that Jesus' relation to the Father, a relation of intimate love—"in the Father's bosom"—brings God out with clarity, literally "exegetes" God whom "no one has seen at any time" (John 1:18).   .

Long ago Augustine identified *caritas* and *cupiditas* as the same exercise of the soul toward different objects.[63] "Love," he writes, "is a kind of craving (*appetitus*)," and "to love is indeed nothing else than to crave something for its own sake." Love and lust for Augustine are the same thing: the former the appetite for a worthy object, the latter the appetite for an unworthy one. *Cupiditas* makes one dependent on that which one can lose against one's will. Augustine follows Plato's understanding of *eros:* Plato has Socrates explain in the *Symposium* that because love is either a desire for something one lacks or the desire never to lose what one has, eros is "always poor" (*Symposium* 203C).

Augustine explains love is a passionate attack on deficiency. We love because we lack. Love is the lack of the beloved. The possession of the beloved is marked by fear: that which was once lacking can be lost again. The desire to have, *appetitus habendi,* turns into a fear of losing, *metus amittendi.* "Love, but be careful what you love," Augustine cautions. This fear remains until the end of time, at the permanent consummation of all things. Only then, reasons Augustine, on the other side of the Eschaton and under the aegis of eternity, will love be without fear.

More recently Paul Tillich also understands love as longing for return to a primordial unity. Thus he ascribes to the understanding of love as deficiency. Ultimately, love is the commitment, or at least the attempt, to overcome the inherent insufficiency of the self: "the drive toward reunion of the separated is love."[64] Tillich acknowledges that this love "is not the Biblical concept of love, which is person-centered, but is love in the sense of the desire for reunion with that to which one belongs."[65] "Agape without eros is obedience to a moral law, without warmth, without longing, without reunion. Eros without agape is chaotic desire, denying the validity of the claim of the other one to be acknowledged as an independent self, able to love and to be loved. Love as the unity of eros and agape is an implication of faith."[66] What Tillich calls the "emotional element," i.e., the erotic, "cannot be separated from love; love without its emotional quality is 'good will' toward somebody or something, but it is not love. This is also true of man's love of God, which cannot be equated with obedience, as some antimystical theologians teach."[67] But the Elder teaches precisely such an equation of love and obedience. He is Christianity's first "antimystical theologian."

But this love is far from any notions of the erotic. First John 4:20 "implies a rejection not only of Docetism but every form of mystical adoration and vision of God that employs religion as a pretext for withdrawing from the demands of the social situation."[68] The issue here is not the love of God or the love of neighbor or an act of love, but love *in se*. *Agapē* is the commitment, through practice, to overcome the contingent insufficiency of one's brother. Love does not begin in a deficiency that gives rise to desire. Perfect love casts out fear precisely because it does away with deficiency.

In his doctoral dissertation Martin Luther King Jr., discussed Tillich's conception of love, making the distinction between agape, which is free of contingency and condition, and other kinds of love.[69] "All love, except agape," argues King, "is dependent on characteristics that change and are partial, such as repulsion and attraction, passion and sympathy. Agape is independent of these states. It affirms the other unconditionally. It is agape that suffers and forgives. It seeks the personal fulfillment of the other."[70]

With this definition of *agapē* King moves from the personal to the political. He makes the radical claim, "Justice has no independent ontological standing. Justice is dependent on love. It is a part of love's activity."[71] *Agapē* makes justice possible. King thus set the intellectual stage for thinking about agape in the realm of politics. *Agapē* can also be the love of comrades, even the love of a politician and his constituency. As Argentine revolutionary and Cuban hero Che Guevara once made the point with humble eloquence, "Let me say, at the risk of seeming ridiculous, that the true revolutionary is guided by great feelings of love."

For King, 1 John 4:8-16 was the quintessential statement of love. King's notion of *agapē* was informed by Nygren's argument for a distinctive, radically disinterested love defined in the New Testament. Yet King profoundly modified Nygren's thinking, broadening and deepening it with political and social dimensions. The beloved community "was the basis of King's ethical argument for integration and his call for world community."[72]

In King's last book, *Where Do We Go From Here: Chaos or Community?*, he calls for a "genuine revolution of values" in which "our loyalties must become ecumenical rather than sectional." This revolution would give rise to "a worldwide fellowship that lifts neighborly concern beyond one's tribe, race, class, and nation . . . a call for an all-embracing and unconditional love for all men."[73] This love, in its profound challenge to global politics and international relations, is that force which all the great religions have seen as the supreme unifying principle of life. Love is the key that unlocks the door which leads to ultimate reality. This Hindu-Moslem-Christian-Jewish-Buddhist belief about ultimate reality is beautifully summed up in the First Epistle of Saint John: Let us love one another: for love is of God: and every one that loveth is born of God, and knoweth God. He that loveth not knoweth not God; for God is love. . . . If we love one another, God dwelleth in us, and his love is perfected in us. Let us hope that this spirit will become the order of the day.

In the light of Nygren's critique, King's prooftext is ill-chosen. His reading cuts against the very grain of particularity that Nygren's analysis highlights. James Washington has charged that "King . . . overlooks critical discussions of Nygren's interpretation, and actually misinterprets Nygren's view at a number of points."[74] As others have observed, however, King's theological method was eclectic, and he was not above overlooking inconvenient contradictions. He appropriated from other thinkers liberally, even superficially, but always in the light of his own theological agenda. Here King parts with Nygren in his evaluation of the rhetoric of 1 John as exclusive and sectarian. For King, it is quite the contrary: universal, international, ecumenical.

King finds the language of 1 John "all-embracing" and "unconditional." King further accents the universal scope of 1 John 4 by dropping its christological language in his ellipsis. Elsewhere King asserted that the *agapē* of 1 John 4 is the highest good that all people have sought throughout the ages: "This principle stands at the center of the cosmos. As John says, 'God is love.' He who loves is a participant in the being of God. He who hates does not know God."[75] *Agapē* is cosmic in scope.

Authenticity and Idolatry

The writer assures his "children" that those who obey God's commandments are God's children (*tekna*), and those who are God's children are victorious over the world: "everyone who is born of God vanquishes the world. And this is the victory—our fidelity. Who is the one who vanquishes the world? He is the one who trusts that Jesus is the Son of God (5:4-5). This is the word of consolation that Jesus leaves with his disciples in the Farewell Discourse of the Gospel of John (John 16:33). Likewise we find the same insistence on obedience to the commandments as the realization of love that we encounter in the Farewell Discourses (John 14:15, 21; 15:10). Here the Elder states the relation of love and the fulfillment of the commandments with epexegetical clarity: "By this we know that we love the children of God when we love God, that is, when we perform his commandments. For this is love for God: that we perform his commandments" (5:2-3). To love God is to do what God commands.

In their obedience the children of God overcome the world (5:4), just as obedience will give Jesus victory over the world in the Gospel of John (John 16:33). "Every injustice is sin, and it is not a fatal sin. We know that everyone who has been born of God does not sin, but the one born of God guards himself, and the evil one does not catch him" (5:17-18). "Fatal sin" is the sin of Cain, the sin of not loving one's brother. Fratricide is the refusal to share one's material wealth with the brother in need. To withhold the means of living is to commit a capital offense against life.

"We know that we are from God, and the whole world wallows in evil" (5:19). The world lies in evil's grip, stands in its power. The world to which the Elder refers is not the created order, but the world of humanity, or more to the point, the world of human depravity. That world, as Clement of Alexandria observed, "is not the creation, but worldly men living in concupiscence."[76] But those born of God do not wallow in sin, are not caught in it. The addressees may defeat sin by watchfulness and intercession. The writer has in mind here the sins he has discussed throughout his teaching: criminal negligence of the brother in need. Those born of God may be guilty of such negligence from time to time, but this sin is not fatal. There is still hope of restoration by the intervention of the vigilant brother, or by one's own vigilance, by attendance upon the ancient pronouncement "from the beginning," its truth, its work, its commandments.

Verses 5:20-21 close with a reminder of the addressees' intimate knowledge of "the true God," that is, authentic God, and a warning against the worship of that which, according to ancient Israelite revelation, is quintessentially inauthentic: idols. The manuscript tradition of *psi* captures the sense of the last sentence of 5:20, "This is the genuine God, that is, having eternal life."[77] Eternal life is not something God gives. Eternal life is what God is.

The final sentence of the tractate, "Little children, guard yourselves against the idols" (5:21), seems to introduce a new discourse on idolatry. The Venerable Bede recognized that this closing exhortation is metaphorical, a warning against "the doctrine of heretics that always lead to death,"[78] and against "the love of money, which is the service of idols."[79] The Reformers, though not entirely disparaging, were not impressed. Luther read the verse as a sentence tacked on for the sake of the weak and immature.[80] Calvin comments, "Although it is a separate sentence, it is nevertheless just as an appendix to the aforementioned doctrine."[81] By any construal, however, it makes for an unceremonious conclusion: the "amen" supplied by the manuscripts of the Byzantine tradition is a liturgically literate attempt to emend the abruptness that would later provoke Calvin's complaint. Rudolf Bultmann thought the entire concluding section of 5:14-21 completely lacking unity, and characterized it as an unhappy later redaction.[82]

There is a thread that binds together the pieces of this discursive patchwork: the question what is true, the question of authenticity. The children of God, commended to authentic faith in giving of themselves and commended to authentic love in giving to each other, are finally commended to the authentic God, who has given them the insight (*dianoia*) to know "the true God" (5:20).[83] Yet even in their authenticity the children of God must ever be on guard against the inauthentic, the false, the idols. As in the Deuteronomic witness to the ancient Israelite tradition of love, mercy, and justice, the exhortation to justice and the promise of God's justice (Deut 16:18-20) concludes with a proscription against the worship of false gods (Deut 16:21-22).

The Qumran literature singles out idolatry for special condemnation, and the language is metaphorical. The "purity of the soul," a fruit of the "Spirit of truth" in Qumran, "detests all the idols of impurity" (1QS 4.5).[84] Priests warned Qumran neophytes that idols were a dangerous abomination. "Cursed be the one who, in order to walk with the idols of his heart while he enters the covenant, yet stumbles in his sins and keeps his intention to backslide. . . . On account of these idols which have caused men to stumble into sin, his lot will be assigned with those who are cursed forever."[85] The *Damascus Document* defines apostates as those "who have put idols in their hearts and who walk in the obstinacy of their hearts" (CD 20.9-10).[86]

These "idols of the heart" are not and cannot be material things in themselves. These idols are private desires, worshiped in the heart's hidden temple. Idolatry is a matter of the *leb*, the Hebrew word of the Qumran texts translated "heart," signifying the disposition of the will. It is often rendered in the LXX as *dianoia*. In 5:20 it is a *dianoia* that the Son of God has given so that the Elder and his addressees may know the true God: Jesus has given the Elder and his little children a heart for God.

Just as the Hebrew sense of *leb* informs the meaning of *dianoia*, so the Hebrew *yada'*, "to know intimately," sets the semiotic tone for the Greek verb *ginōskō*. This intimate knowledge of the true God, the authentic God, is contrasted with the inauthentic gods of idolatry and its contrary *dianoia*. The theme of divine authenticity is thus the crimson thread that binds the varied exhortations of the concluding chapter of 1 John.

"The God of the Bible rejects idols," explains Elaine Scarry, "that is, representations of the divine."[87] The Mosaic commandment against images is a prohibition against representation. Jack Miles comments on the profound effect this prohibition has had on the aesthetics of ancient Israel. Citing the lampoon of idol-makers in Isaiah 44:13-17, Miles writes, "The Bible's own attitude toward art, to the extent that it may be said to have one at all, is an attitude of indifference rising to occasional hostility."[88] Taking Second Isaiah as the normative aesthetic of the Hebrew Bible, Miles asserts, "The Bible does not see writing as the art of writing in the way that it sees sculpture as the art of sculpture . . . [but] insists on seeing the sculptor in every demystifying detail of his work. The product is demeaned by being thus intimately linked to its merely human producer. The Bible never insists on seeing the writer in any similarly demeaning, demystifying way."[89]

But whereas ancient sculpture is, for the most part, representational, the alphabetized script of Isaiah was not and could not be. The hostility of Israelite tradition is not toward plastic arts so much as it is toward representation. To be more precise: Israelite intellectuals were suspicious of all nonhuman representation. A human being could represent—stand in for—another human being, as Aaron does for Moses. A human being could even stand in for God, as Moses does for Aaron and the children of Israel. But the most egregious sin of the children of Israel, which the Prophets and later the Rabbis never allowed anyone to forget, was the fabrication of an inanimate stand-in for their temporarily absent God and his likewise temporarily absent stand-in Moses. The golden calf was not a representation of the foreign god of Egypt; it was, as the text insists, a representation of the absent God of Israel: "Behold, your god who brought you out of Egypt." What outrages God is not that the Israelites represent him as a golden calf—the representation of deity as a bovine animal fashioned from precious metals was au cuorant in the Levant of the time. What outrages God is that the Israelites represented him *at all*.

"The central problem of the biblical God," writes Julia Kristeva, is that "he cannot be seen, named, or represented. That these traits are particularly applicable to His *love* . . . may give the analyst some insight into the infinitely complex question of the Bible's *prohibition of representation*." Representation, the putting forward of the sign in the place of the thing, is prohibited because love cannot be represented. The representation of love is an idol, for there is no stand-in for love; love has no proxy. Love is present, or it is not. It may be present, but it cannot be represented. "The love that the biblical God has for His people is expressed in another way," Kristeva explains. "Ancient biblical texts do not make a great deal of this love, and when they do intimate it exists, they imply that it cannot be represented."[90] The writer inveighs against idolatry directly as his closing salvo as he has inveighed against the representations of love in language: the prohibition against words written and words spoken as representations of love. For the writer, anything but love—concrete, material, freely given and freely shared, from the gut level and from the common purse—is idolatry.

The sending of Jesus and the authenticity of his messiahship, his anointing, is thus tied to the authenticity of the One who sent him. In the discourses of the Elder, the authenticity of the Father grounds the authenticity of the Beloved Community. In the Gospel of John, the authenticity of the Father will be the ground of authenticity of the Beloved Son, Jesus.

THREE

The Spiritual Gospel

The spirit helps me. Now it is exact.
I write: In the beginning was the Act.
　　　　—Goethe, *Faust* 1224–37

The Gospel of John begins with the claim that this is how it all began. It began with the word, the *logos*. The word comes before everything; it is the word before all the words of testimony to follow. The *logos* is thus itself a *prologos*, a word before words.

The Gospel of John is "the spiritual gospel," as Clement of Alexandria dubbed it in the middle of the second century of the Common Era. Centuries later Friedrich Schleiermacher asserted that the Gospel of John is at once the most historical and the most spiritual of the four Gospels. The *logos* is a testimony at once spiritual and historical. The witness of John the Baptizer punctuates the prologue, thus firmly ensconcing the opening of the Gospel in earthly history, not heavenly prehistory. The testimony of John is a part of the beginning of the story, the account, that is, the *logos*. The first chapter of the Gospel opens with words about him, continues with his words, and ends with Jesus' words addressed to some of John's erstwhile disciples. And as we shall see, the first part of the narrative begins in chapter 1 and ends in chapter 10 with the mention of John. And so the prologue, formally 1:1-18, is of a piece with the rest of the first half of the narrative.

The emphasis of the prologue, this word before words, falls on the predicate and not the subject of the *logos*. The prologue of the Gospel of John is an account of the divine word coming to dwell with, in, and through human beings. The *logos* became flesh and dwelt "in our midst," "in us," "with us" (John 1:14): this is the proclamation, the announcement from the beginning. The import of the proclamation, however, is the incarnation "among us," the testimony, in the words of theologian Jo Anne Marie Terrell, of "with-us-ness."[1] The *logos*, taking time to be in that time and taking place in that place, is a very human project. Through this very human project of incarnation, God is immanent in the world.

After the phrase "at the start," there is no hint of Genesis 1 and the creation account. The verbs for "create," "make," "form" are entirely absent. Names, events, and vocabulary point not to the creation of the world in Genesis 1 but to the epiphany at Sinai in Exodus 33-34. The vocabulary of 1:1-14—word, light, life, God, testimony, glory, grace, truth—are reminiscent of the mediation of the Law on Sinai.[2] This accounts for the variant "Lord God" in the original reading of D, where the majority reads "God" for v. 6: "Lord God" is the God of the epiphany at Sinai. It is not strictly Septuagintal: the language is Greek with the accent of the Aramaic targums. The *logos*, according to the targumim, was the mediator of divine revelation there. Philo (*Som.* 1.229) makes a distinction between the *logos*, which he describes as *theos*, "divine," and God, *ho theos*. We may thus render the opening of the narrative, "In the beginning was the word, the divine word."

Though the Word "was," the events of its advent "happened," "came to pass." The account begins with John, not Jesus: the name "Jesus" does not occur until the very end of the Prologue: grace and truth "came to pass" by Jesus Christ. The logos became flesh—not man, but flesh—and dwelt "in us." The incarnation takes place in history and in community. The Word "came to pass"; according to the prologue, its incarnation did not "happen" in Jesus Christ. The incarnation happened "in us."

Verse 18 connects the foregoing summary of events with the words of John placed in a narrative framework. In this way John's testimony becomes a part of Jesus' story. In recounting the Word and the testimony, the narrator has introduced all the actors with leading roles and key supporting roles in the drama: the Word, life in the Word, and the light of people in the life that is in the Word. Then there is John, the Baptist. And "us." Then there is the Law given through Moses, and the mercy and truth that came to pass through Jesus Christ. Then there is John's testimony, the Judeans, the priests and Levites, the Pharisees,

Messiah, Elijah, the Prophet. The narrator cites the words of Isaiah—not the book of Isaiah—as prophetic warrant for John's preaching. The words are not accompanied by the epithet, "it is written": the appeal is to the prophet and not the prophet's book. There is the mysterious man who comes after John and is before him, yet remains unknown to him. And finally there are a few of John's disciples, who become followers of Jesus.

In 1:18 the nouns are without articles, in spite of the long tradition of translation and interpretation that reads "a father" as "the Father" and "a son" as "the Son."[3] It is better rendered, "No one has ever seen God. A dear son, being in the lap of the father, he set things forth." This language of God's bosom, literally God's "lap," is reminiscent of what we find in rabbinic tradition to speak of the Torah's intimate proximity to God. *Midrash on Psalms* 90:3 sec. 12 (Buber 196a) says, "It [Torah] lay on God's bosom, while God sat on the throne of glory." "Through the first-born God created the heaven and the earth," declares *Gen. Rab.* 1,1, commenting on Genesis 1:1, "and the first-born is none other than the Torah." Rabbinic commentary shows that the phrases "in the lap of" and "first-born" are metaphors of proximity, not statements of generation. The "first-born" is a Semitic idiom for being near and dear. The first-born son is, according to Mosaic law, "holy unto the Lord." This was a revolution in the history of Iron Age Canaanite religion, which marked the first-born son for immolation. The first-born was usually sacrificed to the deity, as in the popular cult of Moloch. In Israel, the first-born sons become priests. Instead of becoming sacrifices, first-born sons offered them. According to Deuteronomic legislation treating primogeniture, the first son is born of a hated spouse is still to receive the double portion (Deut 21:15). The son of the beloved wife, called "the first-born," is not literally born first, as the text itself insists. This is exactly the point: the phrase "first-born" indicates affection and proximity, and not order of birth.

Jesus' words and deeds are signs pointing to something beyond themselves. They are metaphors in motion: in the words of Aristotle, whose definition still serves, "Metaphor consists in giving the thing a name that belongs to something else; the transference being either from genus to species, or from species to genus, or from species to species, or on ground of analogy" (*Poetics* 1457b). As metaphors, they are not to be interpreted literally: no metaphor can be reduced to literal usage.[4] Indeed there is a running argument in the Gospel that Jesus' language is understood *pied de lettre* only by those who do not understand him and those who refuse to. Nicodemus makes this mistake (3:1-4). The Galileans also misunderstand the significance of the superabundance of food in the Bread of Life discourse following the mass picnic, and a puzzled Pilate misunderstands Jesus' cagey metaphorical language.

The Gospel of John abstracts proverbial wisdom to metaphor. Jesus uses the agrarian proverbs of harvest as a metaphor for the recruitment of the Samaritans to his project (4:35-38). The saying, "There are yet four months and then the harvest" (4:35), is marked as a proverb by its introduction, "do you not say."[5] The proverb here serves as a metaphor for the ingathering of the Samaritan Israelites.

Some metaphors had already undergone development in Israelite Wisdom and in Israelite apocalyptic before becoming a part of the Beloved Community's semiotic repertoire. The traditional relationship between a father and a son, a commonplace of traditional agrarian society, is used to signify God's relationship to Israel (Hos 11:1), to Israel's king (Psalm 2); but it is the use of the metaphor later in Israel's history to describe God's relation to the faithful righteous that informs the language of the Beloved Community: "the righteous man is God's child, he will help him, and will deliver him from the hand of his adversaries" (Wis 2:17). The father loves the son (John 3:35, 5:20). Those who honor the father honor the son as well (5:23), and the so those who serve Jesus will be honored by his father (12:26). Father and son are one and the same with respect to agency: "I and my father are one" (10:30). Yet the son is subordinate to the father, because his agency is coterminous with the authority of the father: Jesus will later concede to his disciples, "the Father is greater than I" (14:28). In 5:16-30 we encounter proverbial wisdom about the relationship between father and son in a traditional society juxtaposed with an eschatological saying about the Son of Man. The word "son" serves as the lexical link between wisdom saying and eschatological sayings.

Likewise, "above" and "below" or "beneath" are locative adverbs that had become ethical metaphors in Israelite Wisdom centuries before the Gospel was written: "The way of life of life is above to the wise" (Prov 15:24). John 3:31-36 characterizes all those who "come from above," including John the Baptist. There are two orders of being: of things above (*ta anō*) and things below (*ta katō*).

To come from heaven means to come from above. John is "a man sent from God" (1:6), and John's witness is from God; his testimony is thus from above and from heaven.

The prologue is emphatically clear that John, who takes to the stage of the drama well in advance of Jesus, is not the light; John merely bears witness to it (1:8). Later John speaks directly to Jesus—not to those round about, as the singular vocative, "look" (*ide*, 1:29, and again in 1:36) suggests. John explains to Jesus the plan of God as it was revealed to him and as he has explained it in the past. He attests that the one who sent him to baptize, presumably God, has done so to make manifest to Israel the one whom John and all Israel awaits. And though he has seen the spirit light upon him "like a dove," John also attests emphatically that he did not recognize him. He awaits one who comes after him, but he is the first to admit that he does not know for whom he waits.

To John's apologia for his work in the muddy waters, Jesus replies not a word. Jesus is also silent the following day when John repeats himself when he catches sight of Jesus "walking around" where John is gathered with his disciples (1:35-36). John addresses Jesus for the second time, and again Jesus is unresponsive (1:36). Two of John's disciples, however, overhear John's apologia and do what John fails to do: they engage Jesus in conversation (1:37). The two go home with Jesus that day, and subsequently become his first reported disciples. John is thereby unceremoniously stripped of two of his followers.

The Beloved Community did not remember Jesus as a disciple or colleague of John. John does not baptize Jesus. Jesus does not follow John; indeed Jesus does not even speak to John. John "testifies" of Jesus, saying, "I must decrease" (3:30), and with that he will diminish to nothing: this is the last we hear from him. We are summarily notified in 3:24 that John had not yet been thrown into prison. Why would John be arrested and incarcerated? What would be the charges? What was the disposition of his case at the time of the narrative? What of John's disciples? The narrator speaks only of John's imprisonment, and nothing more. John 3:25-29 describes Jesus and his disciples of as baptizing more that the disciples of John, though only a little later the narrator insists that Jesus did not follow or at any time take up John's practice (John 4:1). Jesus' work is different, and that difference receives attention and emphasis elsewhere in the story. Though John did not know for whom he had been waiting, others in Peraea later identify Jesus as that man in an unflattering comparison: "Though John never performed a miraculous sign, all that John said about this man was true" (10:41).

The story addresses the question of Jesus' identity by showing, from the start in Peraea, where he stays, whence he is coming, and whither he is going all over the ancestral regions of Israel. He has personal encounters with people in each of these regions, where he engages them in conversation that is sometimes cryptic, sometimes confrontational, sometimes both. And he will arrive at his final destination by way of both dialogue and travelogue, bidding fellow travelers to "come and see."

FOUR

In Those Parts

This story of Jesus traces a crimson thread that runs through the Law and the Prophets: an ingathering of all the far-flung children of Israel. In the fullness of time the Israelite homeland will gather outcasts from the ends of the world.

> When all these things have happened to you, the blessings and the curses that I have set before you, if you call them to mind among all the nations where the LORD your God has driven you, and return to the LORD your God, and you and your children obey him with all your heart and with all your soul, just as I am commanding you today, then the LORD your God will restore your fortunes and have compassion on you, gathering you again from all the peoples among whom the LORD your God has scattered you. Even if you are exiled to the ends of the world, from there the LORD your God will gather you, and from there he will bring you back. The LORD your God will bring you into the land that your ancestors possessed, and you will possess it; he will make you more prosperous and numerous than your ancestors.
>
> (Deut 30:1-5 NRSV)

God will send his servant to restore Israel's survivors.

> And now the LORD says,
>   who formed me in the womb to be his servant,
> to bring Jacob back to him,
>   and that Israel might be gathered to him,
> for I am honored in the sight of the LORD,
>   and my God has become my strength—
> he says,
> "It is too light a thing that you should be my servant

> to raise up the tribes of Jacob
> and to restore the survivors of Israel;
> I will give you as a light to the nations,
> that my salvation may reach to the end of the earth."
> (Isa 49:5-6 NRSV)

The division of Israel into two kingdoms—the kingdom of Israel in the north and the kingdom of Judah in the south—was damage almost a millennium old that the LORD would nevertheless undo in the fullness of time. The prophet Ezekiel looked forward to a Davidic monarch who would rule over a unified kingdom as had David.

> Thus says the Lord GOD: I will take the people of Israel from the nations among which they have gone, and will gather them from every quarter, and bring them to their own land. I will make them one nation in the land, on the mountains of Israel; and one king shall be king over them all. Never again shall they be two nations, and never again shall they be divided into two kingdoms. They shall never again defile themselves with their idols and their detestable things, or with any of their transgressions. I will save them from all the apostasies into which they have fallen, and will cleanse them. Then they shall be my people, and I will be their GOD.
>
> My servant David shall be king over them; and they shall all have one shepherd. They shall follow my ordinances and be careful to observe my statutes. They shall live in the land that I gave to my servant Jacob, in which your ancestors lived; they and their children and their children's children shall live there forever; and my servant David shall be their prince forever. I will make a covenant of peace with them; it shall be an everlasting covenant with them; and I will bless them and multiply them, and will set my sanctuary among them forevermore. My dwelling place shall be with them; and I will be their God, and they shall be my people. Then the nations shall know that I the LORD sanctify Israel, when my sanctuary is among them forevermore.
> (Ezek 37:21-28 NRSV)

In this sweeping oracle, all of Jacob's children belonged to the commonwealth of Israel as the children of God. The refusal of ancestral Israelites to acknowledge this bond was a feature of Israel's national failure. In his peregrinations through the ancestral lands of Israel and his direct contact with the descendants of the fractured commonwealth, Jesus seeks to overcome these historically rooted hatreds that had caused the project of God to fracture along the fault lines of region and class, ancestry and legacy.

Betharaba, in Peraea

The story of Israel's entry into the Land of Promise begins in the Transjordan: it is the territory on the eastern side of the Jordan that Moses bequeaths to the tribes of Reuben, Gad, and the half-tribe of Manasseh (Joshua 13:8). Though 1 Chronicles 5:26 reports that the Assyrians deported these tribes when King Pul of Assyria conquered the northern kingdom of Israel, down to the Common Era some of the population there were descended from the survivors of that part of the Israelite population that did not go into exile.[1] The Beloved Community's story begins in Peraea, as the Transjordan was called under the Roman imperium, in Bethabara or Betharaba. And it is to Bethabara that Jesus returns at end of the first half of the narrative (10:40-42). Peraea thus geographically brackets Jesus' pan-Israelite itinerary.

On the eastern side of the Jordan River Jesus meets Nathaniel, "an Israelite in whom there is no guile" (1:47). Jesus' salutation alludes obliquely to a prophetic oracle of Israelite restoration that looked forward to a day when God will remove all treachery and deceit from Israel; only those Israelites who are honest and true will remain.

> For I will leave in the midst of you
>   a people humble and lowly.
> They shall seek refuge in the name of the LORD—
>   the remnant of Israel;
> they shall do no wrong
>   and utter no lies,
> nor shall a deceitful tongue
>   be found in their mouths.
> Then they will pasture and lie down,
>   and no one shall make them afraid.
>   (Zeph 3:12-13 NRSV)

These guileless inhabitants will be safe in the land. Jesus greets Nathaniel as one who utters no lies and is not possessed of a deceitful tongue; Nathaniel is one to whom God has promised peace and safety. When Nathaniel inquires how it is that Jesus knows him, Jesus replies that he saw him "under the fig tree" (1:48). This suggests clairvoyance, but of a particular kind. The fig tree is another Israelite figure of safety and security. When the field commander of the Assyrian army tries to persuade the Judeans to surrender, he promises them that if desert king Hezekiah, "... every one of you will eat from his own vine and fig tree and drink water from his own cistern" (2 Kgs 18:31). The fig tree became a topos signifying peace and security in the coming age of Israel's restoration. The prophet Micah predicts that in the last days, "Every man will sit under his own vine and under his own fig tree, and no one will make them afraid" (Mic 4:4). The prophet Joel declares that the LORD will repel invading armies and establish peace in Israel: "Be not afraid, O land; be glad and rejoice. . . . Be not afraid, O wild animals. . . . The trees are bearing their fruit; the fig tree and the vine yield their riches" (Joel 2:21-22). And in Zechariah's oracle of "things to come," the LORD promises, "'I am going to bring my servant, the Branch' . . . says the LORD Almighty, 'and I will remove the sin of this land in a single day. In that day each of you will invite his neighbor to sit under his vine and fig tree,' declares the LORD Almighty" (Zech 3:8-10).

Because Jesus has recognized Nathaniel on sight as an Israelite of integrity, Nathaniel recognizes Jesus on sight as God's Son, the king of Israel (1:49). Jesus replies that Nathaniel will see something greater still: heaven opened and angels coming up to and falling down in the presence of "the son of man," that is, humanity. The safety of the righteous, as other Israelite oracles assert, is to be secured by angels.

> If you make the Most High your dwelling—
> even the LORD, who is my refuge—
> then no harm will befall you,
> no disaster will come near your tent.
> For he will command his angels concerning you
> to guard you in all your ways.
> (Ps 91:9-11)

Angels will attend to the welfare of humanity, and the guileless will dwell in safety. The dialogue carries a double-entendre that tacitly suggests the long-held hopes of Israelite restoration: divinely guaranteed safety for the innocent, the promise of a life of peace in the land that the God of the Israelites had given them so long ago.

Cana, in Galilee

Jesus, having refused John's invitation to baptism in the Transjordan, elects instead to reply in the affirmative to a wedding in Cana, sealing his determination to leave Peraea for Galilee. With a few newly minted disciples in tow, Jesus heads north and west.

When the northern kingdom fell to the Assyrian Empire in the seventh century BCE, the Assyrian intention was to depopulate Galilee, "all the land of Naphtali."[2] Certainly much of the later Hasmonean extension north to Galilee had been accomplished by force. But popular Israelite traditions in Galilee had been woven together in the sacred stories of ancient Israel centuries before they became the ideology of Hasmonean expansionism.[3] Whether by conversion or compulsion, large, Jerusalem-oriented rural populations had developed at the northern end of Palestine in ancestral Israelite territory.

For Jesus, Galilee is the region of miracles: in the narrative, every time he is there something miraculous happens (John 2:1-11; 4:43-54; 6:1–7:9). The first of these miraculous interventions in the narrative, which the narrator calls a "sign," is the wine that Jesus supplies the wedding feast in Cana of Galilee. The traditional northern Israelite wedding feast lasted seven days (see Jud 4:12; Tob 11:19), and by the time Jesus and his entourage arrive the party has exhausted its reserves of wine. Jesus transforms into wine the water in six stone jars used in Judean ritual ablutions, saving the wedding party from social disaster in a feat of miraculous sacrilege by turning consecrated vessels into an open bar. The miracle is the first of several acts of Jesus that show his flagrant disregard for Judean piety in all its forms.

And such acts at the same time point to the realization of ancient Israelite hopes for a coming age of fulfillment and freedom. Classical Israelite prophecy looked forward to an abundance of wine in the time of Israel's restoration.[4] In an oracle of Amos, free-flowing wine marks the time when God will restore the fallen house of David: "The time is surely coming, says the LORD, when . . . the mountains shall drip sweet wine, and all the hills shall flow with it. I will restore the fortunes of my people Israel, and they shall rebuild the ruined cities and inhabit them; they shall plant vineyards and drink their wine. . . . I will plant them upon their land, and they shall never again be plucked up out of the land that I have given them, says the LORD your God" (Amos 9:13-15 NRSV). In the Second Temple period the superabundance of wine was anticipated as a sign of the messianic age. *First Enoch* 10:19 looks forward to the vine yielding wine in abundance, and in *2 Baruch*, a late-first-century apocryphon, each vine shall have

1000 branches and each branch 1,000 clusters (29:5). The wedding feast at Cana is a "sign" that the "day surely coming" has now arrived.

Later after a two-day sojourn in Samaria (4:20, 43), Jesus returns to Galilee. The Galileans receive him with a warm welcome. There in Cana Jesus is accosted by a nobleman from Capernaum who is a *basilikos*, a royal Herodian official. The nobleman is a man of privilege, accustomed to giving orders, accustomed to having his way. The story speaks of a royal official and his entourage of slaves (4:51). The official, as befits his station, comes to Jesus with demands. Jesus rebuffs the official's importunate requests that Jesus come to heal his dying son, and answers the imperative of the official with his own: "Go," perhaps with the sense of "go away." The official demanded that Jesus "go down" to heal his son; but it is then the official who must "go down" at Jesus' behest. The healing is to be accomplished by remote control.

It is the second Galilean sign. The people must see signs to know that the time of Israel's divine restoration is at hand. And so Jesus provides them. The sense of 4:48, "You must see it to believe it," is not pejorative: here Jesus makes an observation, not an accusation. In the prophetic tradition of Isaiah, healing is a root metaphor for communal restoration (Isa 29:18-21; 35:5-6; 42:18-20; 43:8). Healing is signification. The accounts of the physical restoration of infirm persons are signs that point to the activity of God in Israel.

Later during the Passover season, crowds follow Jesus as he returns to Galilee because of "the signs that he performed." Jesus withdraws to the mountains with his disciples to establish some distance between himself and his hostile audiences in Jerusalem. There Jesus oversees an open-air feast for thousands of his followers. The picnic takes place "near the time of the Passover." This is precisely the time that anyone intending to observe the Passover in Jerusalem should have been en route to the city. The Galilean masses here effectively boycott "the feast of the Judeans" to be with Jesus. The notice of the Passover is juxtaposed with that of the crowd "that had come with him" from Jerusalem. The gathering in Galilee is radically different from that about to take place in Jerusalem. No money changes hands at this feast. No animals are sacrificed: the meat of the feast is the flesh of a ritually clean animal never sacrificed—fish. The feast in Galilee promises to be the opposite of the Jerusalem Passover, a counter-Passover: without money, without sacral slaughter, and without the Jerusalem priesthood that oversees the exchange of the one for the other.

Sychar, in Samaria

While baptizing with his disciples in the Judean countryside, Jesus becomes aware of the menacing surveillance of the Pharisees and moves north. His destination is Galilee. The narrator says that Jesus "had to go through Samaria" (4:4 NRSV). But this was not due to the brute fact of geography. Though Samaria lies between Galilee and Judea on the western bank of the Jordan, Israelites from the north who worshipped in Jerusalem were accustomed to crossing the Jordan twice to do an end-run around hated Samaritan territory.

This day, however, Jesus would take the express route. From Judea he proceeds to Sychar, thirty-five miles north of Jerusalem. Sychar, ancient Shechem of the Hebrew Bible and royal capital of Samaria, lies nestled in the valley in the 700-foot shadow of the holy Mount Gerizim, one of Israel's oldest sacred sites. The road from Jerusalem in the south to Samaria in the north runs between Mount Ebal to the north and Mount Gerizim to the south. Long ago history had made of that valley an abysmal chasm.

Less than a half mile from the northwestern side of Mount Gerizim lay Jacob's Well. The ubiquitous Jacob of the patriarchal narratives was the eponymous ancestor of all Israel, as father of the twelve eponymous ancestors of the twelve tribes.[5] The ancient Israelite tribes named after Jacob's sons Ephraim, Manasseh, and Benjamin respectively received what was to become the territory of the Samaritans, who were the descendants of the Israelites that fell to the Assyrian Empire in the seventh century before the Common Era. The Assyrian emperor Sargon II shattered Samaria, which survived as a depopulated rump state. According to his court propaganda, Sargon exiled various Arabian tribes and "settled them in Samerina [*sic*]."[6] "The remnant of those that escaped," as 2 Chronicles 30:6 calls those who fled the Assyrians, continued to live on the western side of the Jordan after the destruction of the northern kingdom. The region assumed the name of its royal capital, Samaria, and its ethnic, religious, and political development followed a course that diverged from that of the Israelites in the southern kingdom of Judea. In 166 BCE on the eve of the Maccabean revolt, Antiochus IV Epiphanes ordered that the Samaritans were not to be punished along with the Judeans because they have proved that 'they are not implicated in the charges against the Judeans but rather "live according to Greek ways.[7] This suggests that customs north and south had become distinctively different even to third parties.

The southern kingdom of Judah fell to the Babylonians a century after Samaria had succumbed to Assyria, and also suffered a deportation of its élite. Some descendants of that élite returned to Judea after the fall of the Babylonian Empire under the patronage of its Persian successor. According to biblical accounts, Marduk commands the Persian emperor Cyrus to restore gods and people to their respective ancestral lands (2 Chron 36:22-23; Ezra 1:1-4; see Isa 45:1-25). Ezra's narrative affords the connection between the "returnees" and the old temple: they brought its treasures with them (Ezra 1:5-11; Dan 1:2; 5:2-4), although elsewhere we learn that those same treasures had been looted and destroyed long ago (2 Kgs 24:13; 25:13-17; 2 Chron 36:19).[8]

The "return" was a creation of a new people with a new cult, centered on a new temple with a Persian administrator of Judean ancestry (Neh 1-11). Under Persian patronage, the Judeans from Babylon established in Judea the cult of the empire's highest divinity, *elohe shamayim*, "the God of the heavens." Second Chronicles 36:22-23 and Ezra 1:1-4 identify *elohe shamayim* with Yahweh, the god of the returnees and the all but forgotten God of Israel.[9] "The people of the deportation," the descendants of those who had been deported with King Jechoniah in 597 BCE, were to constitute the legitimate Temple community. They alone were the "sacred enclave," the "holy community" that must keep itself apart from the people of the land.

The returnees barred the indigenes from their new community, including the descendants of the residual Israelite population left in the land after the deportation. The Persian repatriation of the Judeans in their ancestral homeland would cause a rift deeper and bitterer than the Assyrian and Babylonian deportations.

Josephus reports that in the fourth century BCE the Samaritan ruler Sanballat built a temple on Mount Gerizim to rival that in Jerusalem. At the end of the second century John Hyrcanus, Hasmonean ruler of Judea, would suffer the competition with the Jerusalem sanctuary no longer and burned Sychar and its temple to the ground. The animus between north and south festered on both sides of the border over the centuries and into the Common Era. Josephus's report of a Samaritan attack on Galilean pilgrims to Jerusalem in the mid-first century suggests the Samaritan hostility toward anything and anyone oriented toward Jerusalem. Roughly a decade after the attack, the famous synod of Hillelites and Shammaites ratified a slate of legislation that vilified the Samaritans (*b. Shabbath* 16b).

The narrative of the encounter between Jesus and the Samaritan woman carries with it the ponderous burden of this troubled history, and we cannot appreciate the nuances of the conversation without bringing this background to the foreground. Jesus engages the woman in conversation, and she evinces surprise because she has identified him as a Judean and so assumes his antipathy for her as a Samaritan. Only here in the story are Jesus identified by anyone as a Judean. Nowhere does Jesus so refer to himself and nowhere does anyone so refer to Jesus. Later in the story, Judeans in Jerusalem will be emphatic that Jesus is a Galilean and not one of them. But at the narrative level, for the Samaritan woman, Galilean versus Judean is a distinction without a difference; both groups held the sacral centrality of the Jerusalem Temple. As the Samaritan attack on Galilean pilgrims to Jerusalem in the mid-first century indicates, anyone going to or coming from Jerusalem was, by Samaritan lights, Judean enough.

The scene of the conversation is Jacob's Well. To readers of the Hebrew Bible, romantic innuendo of the scene is unavoidable. In Israelite lore a well was where man found his mate: Isaac (Gen 24:11), Moses (Exod 2:15), and, especially important for this narrative, Jacob (Genesis 29): the whole scene plays upon the topos of betrothal, and is reminiscent of Jacob's meeting of his future wife Rachel in Genesis 29.[10] Jesus' command to the woman to go get her husband is the rhetorical equivalent to the question, "Are you married?"

The conversation takes an abrupt turn in v. 16: the surprise is neither Jesus' command nor the woman's response but Jesus' rejoinder that she has had five husbands. Again, as in his conversation with Nathaniel at the beginning of the story, Jesus makes an apparently clairvoyant pronouncement; and once again the language of the pronouncement makes it more double-entendre than a parlor trick. In ancient Aramaic, "five husbands" translates as "five lords (*ba'alim*)." According to 2 Kings 17:24, people from Babylon, Cuthah, Avra, Hamath, and Sepharvaim became local Samaritan rulers, and Josephus speaks of the five nations that ruled Samaria (*Ant.* 9.14.3). Second Kings and Josephus agree that the Samaritans have been subject to five foreign regimes, five *ba'alim*. Jesus speaks of the five *ba'alim* of the Samaritans, and the sixth *ba'al*, which is not properly a lord but which has nevertheless reduced Samaria to political concubinage under the Roman *imperium* ruling from Jerusalem.

The woman catches the political double-entendre of Jesus' rejoinder and continues the conversation in a political key. The woman waxes chauvinistic. Jesus, after all, is on her turf. And though he appears to know something about her and her people, by her lights Jesus is not the prophet that her people had been anticipating for centuries in accordance with Deuteronomy 18:15-18, the scriptural basis for their expectation of "a prophet like unto Moses." That expectation was fervent at the very moment this story purports to take place. Josephus (*Ant.* 18.85-89) records that just a few years after Jesus was executed, a Samaritan prophet led a large crowd of Samaritans to Mount Gerizim. Pontius Pilate met them at the foot of the mountain with cavalry and heavily armed infantry and slaughtered them, then rounded up those he identified as leaders and executed them. The hapless Samaritans died seeking their savior.

Jesus meets the woman's Samaritan chauvinism with what has been erroneously interpreted as Judean chauvinism of his own. The concluding clause of 4:22 is usually translated, "for salvation is of the Judeans." This purported Judean jingoism "ruptures the context."[11] The verse is more properly rendered, "For it is salvation from the Judeans." Jesus offers deliverance from centuries of Judean antipathy; he speaks of liberation from the enormous ideological and political pressure that Judea had exerted on the Samaritans for centuries. This is the "word" (*logos*) that the Samaritans hear for themselves and receive so enthusiastically.

Passover: Jerusalem, in Judea (2:13-22)

Jesus' attack on the Temple is the main event of Jesus' first swing through Judean territory. In the memory of the Beloved Community, Jesus was opposed to the Temple of Jerusalem, its priesthood, and its cultus that placed itself at the center of the world. It is an interest that ties the prologue to the first half of the narrative. The Gospel of John has no genealogy or birth narrative, and repudiates on principle claims based on blood and descent: "But to all who received him, who believed in his name, he gave power to become children of God, who were born, not of blood or of the will of the flesh or of the will of man, but of

God" (John 1:12-13 NRSV). An established, legitimate pedigree, of course, is one of the requirements for priesthood. And genealogy was the principle on which Israelite "people of the land" were excluded from the commonwealth that Nehemiah, Ezra, and their comrades established in Judea (see Neh 7:5; Ezra 4:1-3).

In 2:15 Papyrus 66 and Papyrus 75 read "something like a whip," and mention sheep and oxen, an attempt to mitigate the violence of the incident: the report is emended to read that Jesus used not a whip but "something like a whip" and, by implication, used it only on the animals. These readings are early spin control on a story in which Jesus is armed and dangerous and physically assaults worshippers and livestock alike. When the pilgrims demand an explanation for his violence, Jesus commands, "Tear down this temple and in three days I will build it up again." The narrator explains, "But he was talking about his body." The narrator also supplies a scriptural warrant for Jesus' violence. The writer has told the story, no doubt already well known to the implied audience, in order to explain it. This suggests that the story, without the gloss and accompanying proof text, was already well known, and that its plain sense—that Jesus launched an armed attack in the Temple and advocated its destruction—was all too plain.

Like the separatists at Qumran, Jesus harbors a dim view of the Temple. But his actions suggest a critique even more radical than that at Qumran. At the northwestern shore of the Dead Sea the dissenting Israelite community established an alternative priesthood, intensified concern for Israelite purity and solidarity, and carried on a vitriolic propaganda campaign against the Jerusalem priesthood. "The Wicked Priest" of the Jerusalem Temple was evil and the cult of the Temple was corrupt; the Qumranites deplored Jerusalem and prophetically anticipated the Temple's divine destruction. But nothing in their tattered literary legacy calls into question ritual purity or priestcraft as such: priesthood and ritual purification were avidly and abstemiously pursued at Qumran. Jesus, by all accounts, was interested in neither priesthood nor ritual purification, and in his attack on the Temple he incites the Jerusalem crowd to do away with both.

But his efforts did not carry the day. Some ancient censor of the tradition introduced this old parenthetical explanation into the account not merely to prohibit a literal reading but also to arrest it. The parenthesis not only prevented naïve readers from reading *à pied de lettre;* it also aspired to stop readers who were already doing so. The parenthesis notwithstanding, the scene shows Jesus in a failed attempt to rally pilgrims to violence against the Jerusalem cult.

The Sabbath (5:1-30)

The three annual pilgrimage feasts are Passover, Pentecost, and Tabernacles. That the feast in question is Passover is a conjecture at least as old as Tatian and Irenaeus. Two other feasts, Rosh Hashanah (New Year) and Purim, have been variously suggested. They are not feasts of pilgrimage, and thus ineligible as a narrative motivation for Jesus to make the trek from Galilee to Jerusalem. Important here is that the feast takes place on the Sabbath.

Careful exegesis fails to establish a baptismal motif here. Indeed this is an anti-baptism: the cripple never gets to the healing waters. He does not even get close, let alone wet. Lying prostrate on the periphery of hope, he is alone in the crowd: his misery has no company. And he is amid destitute masses, "the infirm, the blind, the lame, the paralyzed" (5:4), who congregated near the Temple precincts waiting for the mercy of God or the coins of generous pilgrim passersby. These indigents are beset by disabilities that do not allow their afflictions to go unnoticed. These are Jerusalem Temple's public cripples.

The miracle at the Pool provokes the controversy over Sabbath observance. Jesus slips away "because of the crowd"[12] (5:13) as he does several times in the first half of the narrative (4:41; 7:33; 8:23). After confronting Jesus as an accessory to violation of the Sabbath, the Judeans resolve to kill him (5:17), the first of several notices that some Judeans are plotting Jesus' murder (7:1; 8:37, 40; 11:53). The first half of the narrative is marked by Jesus' evasive maneuvers, suggesting that he changed his residence, kept at a hideout, stayed on the move, sent conflicting signals as to his whereabouts, and exercised great caution when among crowds in Jerusalem (see 5:18; 7:1, 19; 8:37, 40).

The Feast of Tabernacles (7:1–9:41)

The festival of Tabernacles is the autumnal festival celebrating the summer's grain harvest. It was historicized in the Israelite liturgical calendar by its association with the wilderness sojourn after the Exodus (Deut 16:13; Lev 23:34).

In post-exilic times the feast took on eschatological significance. The prophetic oracle of Zechariah 14, that there would be no rain unless the nations did obeisance in Jerusalem, came to be read on the first day of the festival (14:17). Tabernacles celebrates Israel's sojourn in the wilderness (Lev 23:33-34), but Zechariah associates it with eschatological "Day of the Lord" (Zech 14:3) when there will only be light and no darkness, living waters will flow from Jerusalem (14:8), Jerusalem will be exalted (14:10, 14).[13] In the Tabernacles discourse, Jesus claims all this for himself: he is the light, the source of living water; he, not the Jerusalem Temple, shall be exalted.

As the pilgrimage season of the Tabernacles festival approaches, Jesus "was walking around in Galilee because the Judeans sought to kill him" (7:1). But as Jesus' family prepares to go up to the feast, the tension between Jesus and his dubious family and the danger awaiting him in Jerusalem is another occasion for stealth and even dissimulation. In 7:8, where Jesus says, "I am not going to the feast," Papyrus 66 reads "I am not going to the feast *yet.*" Jesus is described in 7:10 as going up to the feast after his family "but in secret." The venerable fourth-century manuscript Sinaiticus and the fifth-century manuscript Codex Bezae both read "as though in secret." The variants of 7:8 and 7:10 attempt to rescue Jesus from appearing to be a liar and a sneak, and we find these apologetical readings among some of the oldest manuscript witnesses.

On the final day of the feast Jesus cries out, "Let anyone who is thirsty come to me, and let the one who believes in me drink" (7:37-38 NRSV). The narrator tells us that Jesus "said this about the Spirit, which believers in him were to receive" (7:39 NRSV). The Feast of Tabernacles was also associated with the promise of "living" (that is, flowing in contrast to standing) waters. According to the Talmud, each morning of the festival, water drawn from the Siloam stream to the south of Jerusalem was brought to the Temple in a joyful procession and poured out on the altar (*m. Sukk.* 4:9-10). The torchlight the night before the procession came to be called "the Joy of the Place of Water-Drawing" (*m. Sukk.* 5:1-5 and *t. Sukk.* 4:1-9).[14] In rabbinic reflection the water imagery of Isaiah 12:3, associated with the Feast of Tabernacles (*b. Sukk.* 48b; 50b; *y. Sukk.* 5:1 [55a]),[15] was symbolic of the Holy Spirit. "R. Joshua ben Levi said: Why is it [the Temple courtyard] called 'the place of Water-drawing'? Because from it they draw out the Holy Spirit, as it is said, 'With joy you will draw water from the wells of salvation' [Isa 12:3]" (y. *Sukk.* 5:1 [55a]). R. Joshua is a first-generation Amora (early third century CE), but the association of water and spirit was already in classical Israelite prophecy (Isa 44:3; Joel 2:28; Ezek 36:25-26) and continued in the intertestamental period (*Jub.* 1:23-25; 1QS 4:19-21).[17]

Among the crowd at the feast is the mass of Jesus' followers from Galilee, and, presumably, his family. The leaders as a group are distinguished from the Jerusalemite masses (7:26). Mentioned specifically are the chief priests and the Pharisees (7:45-48), who act as a police force that unsuccessfully attempts to apprehend Jesus (7:32-36). Nicodemus is a dissenting voice among them (50). Jesus' cryptic conversation with Nicodemus earlier (3:1-21) suggests at the same time a befuddled and diffident sympathy on the part of some Jerusalemite non-priestly elites. Jesus was driving a wedge into the fissure in the post-exilic ruling class in Jerusalem along priestly and non-priestly lines the antique beginnings of which we may discern as far back as Nehemiah's struggle with the Jerusalem priesthood among the repatriated Judeans in the Persian period (see Neh 13:15). We may observe similar tensions between the Hasmonean priesthood and the Pharisees. Clearly, the Judeans hostile to Jesus are the Jerusalemite rulers (7:26; 9:22; 19:38) whom commoners, including Judean commoners, fear. But the narrative also suggests that Jesus is applying pressure to a political fault line of some vintage that runs through the Jerusalemite elite, and that Jesus enjoyed muted support in the ranks of its non-priestly wing.

The Judeans are divided, and they are divided over Jesus. That the people of Judea are divided over Jesus is an important feature of the narrative. At the end of the discourse on the bread of life there is a great defection from Jesus and a consolidation of his inner circle, a division provoked by Jesus' words. "These words" of Jesus cause dissent and disaffection: Jesus' deeds attract the masses, but his words repel them. This is so in Galilee in the synagogue in Capernaum, where his audience is repelled by his words about the bread of life. This is especially so in Jerusalem. The dispute concerning testimony in 8:12-20 hearkens back to the controversy with the Judeans in 5:31-48. Here they are specifically the Pharisees. Likewise 8:21 returns to the argument with the Pharisees in 7:34-36. At the same time, the narration speaks of Judeans who have believed in Jesus (8:33).

The controversy amid the Jerusalem crowd in chapter 7 was a conflict of opinions about Jesus' natural origin, and whether this disqualified him from being a prophet. In chapter 8 Jesus sharpens the point of his argument that his identity is based on what he does, and it is what he does that marks him as the Father's emissary in the world. The Father is ever with Jesus in the world (8:29) because Jesus does what the Father has sent him to do and says what the Father has sent him to say. Jesus is one with the Father in that he speaks the words that the Father has taught him to say, and does the things that the Father has directed him to do.

Jesus is speaking to those Judeans "who had had confidence in him" (8:31). The perfect participle indicates that these Judeans had put their trust in Jesus at an earlier time. Is the point of the notice that their erstwhile confidence no longer obtains? The wrangling of the Judeans then devolves to a flatfooted, ironic denial of history. When Jesus offers his interlocutors freedom, they spit back, "We are descendants of Abraham and have never been slaves to anyone" (8:33 NRSV). God had told Abraham that his progeny would be slaves in Egypt, and Israel's oldest collective memory is the story of their divinely engineered escape of Abraham's descendants from slavery. The irony, here and throughout the narrative, is at the expense of Jesus' adversaries.

What follows is a knot of nasty accusations. The first half of the narrative is punctuated with accusations against Jesus. He is evil (7:12; 9:16, 24; 10:21, 33) or deranged (2:17; 7:20; 8:48, 52; 10:20). Jesus contests the charge of being possessed (8:48-49), but passes over in silence the accusation of being a Samaritan—a slur in Jerusalem. Jesus is compared with Abraham (8:53) just as he is compared to Jacob (4:12), that is, negatively. Yet Jesus insists on his preeminence over the dead past: "I am to be before Abraham" (8:58). This is consistent with the general meaning of Jesus' "I am" statements, in which he contrasts himself to some illustrious figure in the past or the future, insisting on the importance of his own presence.

Zechariah's oracle of "Day of the Lord" foresaw a future of perpetual light. Later the Mishnah *Sukkoth* 3 and 4, dating from the end of the second century of the Common Era, describes waving boughs of palm, myrtle, willow, and citron during the Tabernacles festival while reciting a Hallel psalm: "The LORD is God, and he has given us light. Bind the festal procession with branches, up to the horns of the altar" (Ps 118:27 NRSV). Jesus takes up the seasonal theme of illumination: "I am the light of the world. The one who follows me shall in no way walk in darkness" (John 8:12). We find here in the mouth of Jesus the Beloved Community's language of walking in the light "as he is in the light" (1 John 1:7). Light is a metaphor of justice in classical Israelite prophecy, signifying deliverance and the dawn of a just order (see Isa 9:2; 49:6; 60:1). Thus the discourse of light plays on the feast's association with light, followed with the narrative of the healing of a blind man: "I must do the deeds of him who sent me, while it is day; a night comes when no one can work" (John 9:4); "When I am in the world, I am the light of the world" (9:5); "I have come into the world in judgment, that those who do not see would see, and that those who see would be blind" (9:39).

The Feast of Dedication: The Good Shepherd (10:1-42)

The narrative jumps from the season of the Feast of Tabernacles in the fall to the Feast of Dedication in the winter. Dedication or Hanukkah is an eight-day feast, which commences in winter (25 Kislev, that is, in November or December) and commemorates the rededication of the Jerusalem Temple after the victory of the Maccabees (1 Macc 4:52-59; 2 Macc 10:5-8). Jesus is depicted as being present but not as a participant: once again, the feasts mark narrative time and not Jesus' observance. Dedication hearkens back to a time of crisis in Israelite history when the priesthood and aristocracy were complicit with the enemies of the Torah. The Jerusalemite priestly elite and their non-priestly sympathizers and retainers apostatized in support of the Syrian monarch Antiochus IV Epiphanes.

Here Jesus repeats this accusation of priestly apostasy in earshot of the Jerusalemite élite of his own day. Jesus' words here recall Ezekiel's imagery of the good shepherd as virtuous leader—one of Israel's oldest political metaphors.

> I myself will be the shepherd of my sheep, and I will make them lie down, says the Lord God. I will seek the lost, and I will bring back the strayed, and I will bind up the injured, and I will strengthen the weak, but the fat and the strong I will destroy. I will feed them with justice. . . .
>
> Therefore, thus says the Lord God to them: I myself will judge between the fat sheep and the lean sheep. Because you pushed with flank and shoulder, and butted at all the weak animals with your horns until you scattered them far and wide, I will save my flock, and they shall no longer be ravaged; and I will judge between sheep and sheep.

I will set up over them one shepherd, my servant David, and he shall feed them: he shall feed them and be their shepherd. And I, the LORD, will be their God, and my servant David shall be prince among them; I, the LORD, have spoken.

(Ezek 34:15-16, 20-24 NRSV)

Ezekiel describes David here not as a king but as one who will be a "prince," *nasi*, among them. Jesus, the good shepherd, is the *nasi* that God is using to bring together the scattered flock of Israel.

Later, Jesus again claims unity with the Father (10:30), and again defends himself against the charge of blasphemy and its capital penalty. The narrative revisits the controversy of 5:18, where the Judeans sought to kill Jesus because his claim of divine paternity was understood as an arrogation to equality with God. In chapter 5 Jesus based his defense on the proverbial relation of father and son: the father disclosed his "works" to the son, and the son, in imitation of the father, performed those works: the righteous man is God's child (Wis 2:12-24). This is the argument of the Gospel of John *in nuce*—not that Jesus was God's son and so righteous, but that Jesus was righteous, and so God's son.

Again in chapter 10, the argument for divine sonship is not a defense of a "high christology." It is a defense against the accusation of "high christology," an argument that brings high christology down to earth, as it were. The emphasis here is on beating the charge of blasphemy, and so Jesus adduces Psalm 82:6, a biblical text that offers a precedent for human claims to divinity. The point of the scriptural citation is to show the Judeans' accusation to be a non-issue. But the Judeans violently disagree, become violently disagreeable, and Jesus once again beats a hasty retreat from Judea, this time back across the Jordan to Bethabara in Peraea.

Across the Jordan to Bethany (11:1-44)

Jesus leaves the safety of Peraea to venture back into Judea. He does so for love. Jesus loved Lazarus and his sisters. Martha and Mary loved their brother. And in love they all meet at the grave. Lazarus, in disease and death, succumbs to the last failure of the human condition—the failure to live. In their disappointment Martha and Mary are two women twice deserted. In death, the ultimate desertion, their brother has deserted them. And in their time of desperation Jesus has deserted them.

The crowd comes to the tomb in despair. And Jesus comes, belatedly, in guttural dread. Jesus has left his safe house in the Transjordan to return to the danger of Judea. The setting of public mourning has made secrecy impossible. Jesus is deeply disturbed—the verb elsewhere describes anger or fury—at the same time angered and anguished, because Lazarus's resurrection forces him to compromise his own security. Jesus must operate openly in dangerous territory, mere kilometers from Jerusalem. The resurrection of Lazarus must be spectacle as well as miracle.

Due to the stress that accompanies his grief or grief that accompanies his stress, Jesus becomes undone. "Jesus wept" (11:35). There is no artful monologue here. The prose is taut, spare. The notice is plosive, as if to suggest that Jesus is overcome in an instant in a paroxysm of sobbing. The language of the text, as the emotion it tersely conveys, is sudden and poignant.

Then Jesus, just as suddenly, takes possession of himself and thence the situation. By name he calls forth his beloved friend from death. But by bringing Lazarus back to life, Jesus seals his own doom: the plot to kill Jesus in Jerusalem begins in earnest in response to his overwhelming popularity as a result of the resurrection of Lazarus.

The Anointed (11:45—12:8)

Though the anointing at Bethany is not reported until 12:3, it is anticipated in 11:2, where Mary is introduced as the woman who anoints Jesus. The implied audience already knows this story. Jesus defends Mary's actions. "Allow her so that she may keep it [i.e., the aromatic oil] for the day that I have been embalmed" (12:7). The narrator indicts Judas's complaint as motivated by greed; Judas holds "the money box," *glōssokomon*. In the New Testament the word occurs only in the Gospel of John. It appears four times in LXX of 2 Chronicles 24 as the repository of the fund for temple repairs. This word is used for the common purse of Jesus and his disciples; yet another suggestion of the anti-Temple orientation of Jesus' activity. The Temple treasury now belongs to Jesus and his followers.

Jesus is opposed to augmenting the common treasury by selling the spike-nard, and instead insists that Mary be allowed to keep it for use after he is dead. This has no bearing on Mary's present use of the spikenard. Mary is not embalming Jesus. Because Jesus is not yet dead, he is not being anointed for burial. He is being anointed for something else. Apparently she is in possession of such a quantity of the precious ointment that even after anointing Jesus now there promises to be enough left over to anoint Jesus later. And so Jesus speaks of what she may do with the remaining oil later. The question remains, what is she doing now?

Mary anoints Jesus in the suburb of Bethany just before his triumphal entry into Jerusalem. The Passover was approaching, the crowds in Jerusalem were growing, and the throngs of people had Jesus' name on their lips. There was the popular expectation that Jesus, the man who had called a dead man back to life, would be present at the feast to receive the adulation of his many admirers. The chief priests of Jerusalem and the Pharisees shared this expectation, and they had issued an All Points Bulletin in the hope of apprehending Jesus in Jerusalem during the holidays (11:57).

Suspecting their designs, Jesus stays out of Jerusalem and remains in the suburban villages, Ephraim (11:54) and Bethany (12:1), where the Bethanians throw a party in Jesus' honor. Martha is the party's hostess (12:2), and her brother Lazarus was one of those who reclined at table with Jesus. The other member of Jesus' beloved Bethanian family, Mary, anoints Jesus at the party. It is after his anointing, and the narrator's brief report of that the priests have now decided that Lazarus too should also be murdered, that Jesus enters Jerusalem to public acclaim. The narrative sequence of the Gospel of John shows Mary's anointing of Jesus to be what it had been in Israel for more than a millennium—a political act. Anointing is the Israelite ritual that marks a king. In Bethany, Mary presides over the coronation of Jesus: at her hand, he becomes Messiah.

Jesus arrives in Jerusalem a week before the Passover, when merchants, moneychangers, and priests are already attending to the rush of pilgrims that would clog the city in its holiest festive season. The crowds that welcomed Jesus were the first wave of a flood of humanity that would increase the city's population ten fold. Some of these people greet Jesus with palm branches that they waved aloft in celebration of his entry into the city. The palm frond was an ancient symbol of Israel's liberation. The Israelites had waved palms of victory two centuries before as victorious Israelite troops, having repelled their Syrian enemies, entered Jerusalem in triumph, and purified the Temple that had been desecrated by the Syrians. In both revolts against Rome, the first a generation after the crucifixion of Jesus and the second a century after his crucifixion, the Judean rebels would mint coins with the image of palm fronds and the legend reading "The Liberation of Israel."

The palms waving in the air on either side of the road signified that his hour of exaltation had come. The people finally got it. This was the fourth time in the narrative that Jesus enters Jerusalem in the course of his public career. But only here does he receive a royal reception. After witnessing the lame walk, the blind see, and the dead escape the grave, the people were convinced that God was working out the salvation of the dispersed children of Israel, all Israel, through Jesus.

Many commentators have recognized the acclamation "Hosanna," literally "save us," as an echo of the Hallel Psalm 118:25-26: "O LORD, save us; O LORD, grant us good success. Blessed is he who comes in the name of the LORD." It is a prayer offered traditionally at the Feast of Tabernacles, where palm fronds are used to fashion the huts from which the festival takes its name. The acclamation is also a public plea for royal relief that we find elsewhere in the Bible, where common people approach the king for help. In 2 Samuel 14:4 a Tekoan woman sent by David's general Joab hails David with the salutation "Help me, O king!" During the Syrian siege of Samaria reported in the second book of Kings, a desperate woman calls out to King Azariah, "Help me, my lord the king!" (2 Kings 6:26). "Hosanna" signifies the venerable practice of subjects calling out to their king for relief from distress. The French used to greet their monarch with the acclamation "Long live the king"—until they killed him—and the British still sing, "God save the Queen." But "Hosanna" means "O king, save us." It is a shout of acclamation as a cry for help. The people in Jerusalem seek, and see in Jesus, liberation from their oppressors, just as the Samaritans looked forward to liberation (*sōtēria*, 4:22) from the Judeans. "The Hallel," the Rabbis would later command, "is not read except on the overthrow of a kingdom" (*Pesiq. Rab.* 2.1).

Only now does Jesus mount a young donkey in fulfillment of the oracle of the king's advent in Zechariah 9:9. The language of this scene is based on Israelite oracles of the restored monarchy. Now the Judeans receive Jesus as a king in "the city of the great king," in Jerusalem. Jesus comes as king because the people recognized him as king. The language of this scene is based on an Israelite oracle of the restored monarchy: "Rejoice greatly, O Daughter of Zion! Shout, Daughter of Jerusalem! See, your king comes to you, righteous and having salvation, gentle and riding on a donkey" (Zech 9:9).

The tumultuous reception of Jesus in Jerusalem on the eve of the Passover is his exaltation. The Jerusalem pilgrims exalt an anointed "son of man." He is "lifted up," *naśa*, the verb signifying exaltation, especially of one who is humble or formerly humble or humiliated (Ps 102:10; 147:6; Isa 42:2). One so exalted is a *nasi*, often translated as "prince." Jesus, as one who is lifted up, is Israel's *nasi*. Now the Judeans receive Jesus as a king in "the city of the great king," Jerusalem.

FIVE

Love in extremis
The Farewell Discourses (13:1—17:27)

The intimate dinner party in Jerusalem that serves as the venue for Jesus' farewell to his disciples is not a celebration of the Passover. Here as throughout the Gospel of John, Jesus does not celebrate any of the feasts of the Jerusalem cult. The Gospel never depicts him or any of his disciples as offering sacrifices, and he attends festivals only to take advantage of the populous audience that they afford him. The festivals are markers of narrative time and moments of conflict.

Nor is this meal the inauguration of the Eucharist. There is no upper room. There are no words of institution. Here the bread is not Jesus' body. The wine is not his blood.

Jesus commands his disciples to wash each other's feet. This humble act of love is dirty work. Foot washing is a service customarily rendered by a slave. But the Gospel of John avoids the language of slavery to describe discipleship, and Jesus explicitly rejects slavery as a metaphor. All the proverbial sayings about slaves in the Gospel of John are pejorative. "The slave does not remain in the house forever, but the son does" (8:35); "The slave does not know what his master does" (15:15); "The slave is not greater than his master" (15:20). Jesus is not an obedient slave; he is an obedient son. His followers are not his slaves; they are his "little children."

Jesus calls what he does "an example," a *hypodeigma*, something demonstrated to be imitated. This is the *imitatio Christi* of 1 John 2:6 in the mouth of Jesus. With the emulation of his demonstration, Jesus claims, comes beatitude. This blessedness comes not on the basis of what one knows, but what one does.

The phrases "lean upon the bosom" in 13:25 and "Satan entered into him"

(NRSV) in 13:27 are not to be interpreted literally, but like the phrase "in the lap of the Father" in the prologue, reflect idiomatic Semitic speech. "The one who leaned upon Jesus' breast" is the one closest to him at table. That Satan "entered into" Judas does not mean that Judas was possessed; the Gospel of John, which has neither exorcisms nor demonology, does not understand Satan's work in the world with the ideation of spirit possession. The verb "enter into" also means "share in," "have a part in": after Jesus gave Judas the morsel of bread, the Adversary had a share in what Judas would do henceforth.

The foot washing is not hindered by the imminent betrayal of Judas, foretold in 13:11: he is present until the end of the meal in 13:30, and so presumably has his feet washed along with the others, even though he is not "clean." The language of clean and unclean is cultic, but its spirit is far from the letter of the Temple or other cult. The meaning of Satan's involvement is set out in 13:30: "Having then received the morsel, he [i.e., Judas] went out immediately. And it was night." One in whom Satan is at work is washed in a humble act of love, yet remains unclean. One in whom Satan is at work takes the bread shared in intimate fellowship, then deserts the community, and walks in darkness.

The mystery, the sacrament of the Beloved Community, is the Word dwelling "with us, in us, among us" (John 1:14). The most egregious transgression of community is desertion, "going out"—the rupture of community. Judas is the arch-traitor who "went out" (13:30) into darkness. Those who go out are those who betray the community's generosity and confidence is to walk in darkness, as the Elder puts it (1 John 1:6; 2:11). For those who go out, there is only darkness: "it was night." The report of the other disciples' interpretation of events as onlookers adds an element of irony to the betrayal. Judas held the common fund for the common good: providing for the needs of the group and the needs of the poor were the only two line items on the budget of Jesus' inner circle. He who single-handedly held their goods in common single-handedly destroyed the common good.

Jesus has loved his followers so that they may love each other. Love calls for love in turn. Love makes love imperative. This love is further defined as the concrete concern for the beloved that Jesus has for his inner circle. The members of the Beloved Community are to live for each other the way Jesus has lived for them: they are to put their souls at each other's disposal. Jesus shares with his intimate followers his bread from the heart, and declares as his last will and testament the command that they do likewise for each other. Through his actions Jesus has given love a new definition; thus the commandment is new, the "new commandment" of 1 John 2:7 and 2 John 5, simply "his commandment" in 1 John 3:23. In the Gospel, the commandment comes from the mouth of Jesus.

"Let not your heart be troubled: believe in God, believe also in me" (14:1). As in chapter 11, the verb, "to deeply disturb, trouble" *(tarassein)*, links Jesus' love with the anxiety, danger, and betrayal that come with love. The love of Jesus is not made manifest in the world without provoking the hatred of those who do not know that love and falling prey to the betrayal of those who do. At the risk of hatred and betrayal those who love God keep God's commandments, and those who love Jesus keep his commandments: 14:15 presents the rigorous definition of love that defines the Beloved Community. The writer insisted, "This is the love of God, that we keep his commandments" (1 John 5:3). Anyone claiming to know Jesus who does not keep his commandments is a liar (1 John 2:4). The other "advocate" that the Father will give is the spirit of truth; Jesus himself is thus an "advocate" of his followers (1 John 2:1). The presence of the spirit of truth is at the same time both perennial and conditional. It remains with the "little children" of Jesus insofar as they keep the commandments of Jesus.

The spirit of truth remains with the followers of Jesus because of what they do, insofar as what they do is faithful to the words, the *rhemata* of Jesus. The theme of remaining has already appeared in 5:38 and 8:35, and will be prominent in the Farewell Discourse (14:17; 15:1-18). John 12:34 introduces the double-entendre of "remain." Jesus' first two disciples ask where he is staying (1:39). The Samaritans beseech Jesus to stay two days (4:40). Several transitional passages mention where Jesus "remained" (2:12, in Capernaum; 7:1-9, in Galilee; 10:40-42, in the Transjordan; 11:54, in Ephraim "near the wilderness"). Though Jesus "spent time" in Judea (3:22), verb "remain" is never used of Jesus' visits to Jerusalem. We encountered the theme in the discourses of the writer (1 John 2:14, 27; 3:9, 15, 17, 24; 4:12, 15, 16).

"I will no more speak much with you. . . . Arise, let us go hence." (John 14:30-31). With these words we might expect the words, the *rhemata* of Jesus, to come to an end. If this concluding imperative were then followed by 18:1, the narration would flow smoothly from the Farewell Discourse to the passion narrative. But Jesus' commands and bequests raise issues that yet remain ill defined and unresolved. And so Jesus' testamentary speech becomes an occasion to define and resolve the words of Jesus with more words of Jesus. The words of chapters 15, 16, and 17 carry Jesus' promises, warnings, and instructions forward into the frightening future. These promises, warnings, and instructions themselves become a part of the bequest.

Jesus promises, "Because I go for my father, whatever you ask in my name I would do so that the father would be glorified in the son" (14:12b-13). We find similar phrases in 15:16, "whatever you ask the Father in my name he would give to you," and again in 16:23, "whatever you ask the Father in my name he will give to you." The repeated reworking of Jesus' promise of divine assistance testifies to the anxiety of those to whom that promise is addressed. These sayings describe the means by which the Father will sustain Jesus' "little children" in a hostile word.

Just as the foregoing treats what the Father will do for the followers of Jesus, so the discourse that follows treats what the Father will do to them, as it were. Yet another metaphor, the discourse of the true vine is an image of cultured fecundity, fruit brought forth by diligent husbandry. In Jeremiah's parable of viti-culture (2:21), the "true" vine is the cultivated vine. John 15:1-6 are a statement of the metaphor, vv. 7-17 its explanation. It is a metaphor of fruitfulness. Jesus has chosen his followers to be abundantly fruitful (15:16). The vine is a venera-ble image of fecundity,[1] drawn from ancient Israelite wisdom and a symbol of the usufruct messianic age in the semiotic thesaurus of the classical prophets (see Isa 5:1-7; 27:2-6; Ezekiel 17). But the language here is not eschatological: that is, it does not speak of the end of the age. The metaphor is expressed in the proverbial present tense. The vine is not a figure of hell or judgment at the end of time. This is not about life after death; it is about death after life.

The metaphor of the true vine signifies love as acts of tending, of ongoing tender and not-so-tender cultivation. In the vineyards of northern Palestine fruitless branches are removed from late February to mid-March, and by late March the vines are virtually naked, and fires burning the discarded branches dot the Kidron Valley. In August the vinedresser pinches off errant shoots of the now usufruct branches so that they receive the full benefits of sun and soil. The *logos*, the word, works on the disciples to cleanse them, that is, purge them of unfruitful growth. The branch is an extension of the vine. The vine is indispen-sable for the branch.

The branch, however, is not indispensable to the vine. Tended branches make fruit: untended branches take it. An unfruitful branch compromises the vitality of the vine. Though alive, the branch is not well because it is not fruitful, and thus its very vitality compromises the fecundity of the vine. Unfruitful branches divert nutrients from those that are fruitful and burden the vine. The excised, erstwhile living branches, separated from the vine on which they had imposed for life, now dry up and die, withering and fit only for the tinderbox. The "words" (*rhemata*, 15:7) of Jesus, words of command, effect the pruning process in the common life of his followers.

"The law of love," insisted Reinhold Niebuhr, "is not obeyed simply by being known. Whenever it is obeyed at all, it is because life in its beauty and terror has been more fully revealed to man."[2] In the phrase "that you bear much fruit and that you be my disciples" (15:8), the word "and" is epexegetical: to be a true follower of Jesus is to be exceedingly fruitful. The very purpose of his disclosures is joy (15:11). It was for the sake of joy that the writers have written up the discourses of the writer (1 John 1:3), and it for this reason that the Elder hopes to speak "mouth to mouth" to those to whom he writes (2 John 12). It is joy to make love known in the world.

Yet Jesus anticipates that the world will hate his followers (15:18). It is a collateral hatred—hatred that is the occupational hazard of love. Because the world has hated Jesus, it hates those who are his (15:20-24). For this reason, the writer advised his addressees not to be surprised by the world's hatred toward them (1 John 3:13). Those who belong to Jesus will suffer that hatred in solidarity with him. "You will no longer watch me" (John 16:10), that is, the disciples will no longer be spectators of Jesus' tribulation. The world will become a place of tribulation for them as well.

"This world" is the present regime, and the ruler of this regime has been judged (16:11). And though he comes and interrupts Jesus' converse with his followers, he has nothing to do whatsoever with Jesus and no claim on him (14:30). The word "ruler" here, also translated as "prince," is the Greek word used to render the Hebrew *nasi*—as we have seen, a political term. There is no indication that Jesus is talking about Satan here; on the rare occasions he does so, he does so openly. And there is nothing in the narrative to suggest that Jesus or the narrator understands Satan as the ruler of the world. "This world" is the partnership of the Judean temple state and the Roman imperium in Palestine. The "ruler of this world" is neither Satan nor any of "the rulers of the Judeans." The singular ruler can be only one person: Pontius Pilate. Jesus prophesies that he shall be thrown out (12:31): indeed, Pilate was deposed only a few years after he executed Jesus.

The prophetic image of labor pains that we find in the prophets (Isa 26:17-18; 46:7-10; Hos 13:13; Mic 4:9-10) does not figure in an end-time tableau here. Thus the Gospel of John is not apocalyptic; missing from Jesus' last discourses is any hint of the Synoptic apocalypse. For the same reason there is no sudden revelation of Jesus at the transfiguration: Jesus is fully manifest throughout his life in the world. Jesus is manifest to the world in his work now, and the tribulation of the end of the present regime is the tribulation of the present.

Jesus' followers will not have tribulation because the present regime is dying. They will have tribulation because a new regime is being born. And the new regime is coming into the world the way all new human life comes into the world: with fitful pains at times so agonizing that they threaten life itself. Childbirth has always been potentially lethal for women. Yet the woman in labor rejoices after her travail is over. The cause for her joy is not the cessation of her pain, but what that pain has wrought—new human life. Jesus does not say that she forgets that pain, just as women who have gone through labor do not forget the experience. What Jesus says, however, is that the woman does not *remember* the pain. The root of the word "remember" here is cognate to the word for "memorial" and "tombstone," mnemonic devices that mark the dead past in the living present. The woman's joy is at the same time the celebration of new life and a refusal to commemorate past agony. Joy, ever predicated on suffering, is the death-defying affirmation of life.

Jesus concludes his bequest, as do all the great testators of ancient Israel, with a prayer. Chapter 17 is a prayer for those who keep the word, the *logos* of Jesus. The prayer is comprised of three petitions. In the first petition, Jesus prays for his own glorification (17:1-8). There is an implicit difference in the Gospel between the glorification of God, manifest in the signs that Jesus performs, and the glorification of Jesus himself, to which the proleptic notice in John 12:16 refers. Jesus describes his own activity as having glorified the Father by completing the work that the Father has given him to do. Completely absent here is the language of sacrifice, and there is no mention of the cross. Nor is there any hint of sin or vicarious atonement. It is only after Jesus' suffering, death, and resurrection that his followers make sense of his words and deeds; on the eve of his death, however, death is a non-issue.

Glory is recognition based on what one has done. Honor is recognition by dint of what others say. Though the people in the world may honor Jesus, and though they may exalt him and "lift him up" as a ruler, only God can give him glory. It is in the midst of his disciples that he receives glory. It is in the midst of his disciples that he returns to the Father, that he reveals the Father's glory, and that he speaks plainly. For Jesus to be in the midst of his own and the Father's own is to be "out of the world." Outside this inner circle of love, Jesus does not reveal the Father's glory. The references here are neither locative nor temporal. "The world" is the totality of the present regime. The world does not and cannot know the love shared among those who belong to the Father; it may only be revealed to those whom the Father has given to the Son.

In the second petition of his prayer, Jesus intercedes for his disciples (vv. 9-19). Eternal life is not the knowledge of God but the ongoing act of knowing the only true God. From the mouth of Jesus comes an affirmation of the writer's teaching that God is eternal life (1 John 5:20). The Elder also taught that the entire world is lies in the power of evil (1 John 5:19). Jesus petitions the Father that he would keep the disciples in the world and out of the grip of evil, that they might remain in the world and not of it (John 17:15-16).

Nevertheless those that belong to Jesus may share their joy with each other in the hostile world, and so Jesus asks that they might have this joy in all its fullness. Just as Jesus has been consecrated to the work of Father, he now consecrates others to do that work. The verbs "consecrate," and "sanctify" and their cognates here have nothing to do with the language of sacrifice. Jesus has not consecrated his followers to die, but to live—for the Father, for him, and for each other. And so there is no mention of death here. Even the threat of death that Jesus discusses in chapter 16 fades in the brilliant hope of divine safety that Jesus' intercession seeks to secure. Those whom Jesus consecrates are set aside to be safe in a dangerous world, to be joyful in a sorrowful world, to be loved in a hateful world. So commissioned, they are sent out just as Jesus was sent out.

In the third and final petition Jesus prays for those who will put their trust in his word (vv. 20-27). Others are added to the small, beleaguered circle that eavesdrops on Jesus' prayer. They are the "other sheep" of chapter 10, including the implied readers, among others. They, with the disciples and Jesus and the Father, are all to be one. Though each is distinct and discrete, "being one" means that all are one in word and work. Just as Jesus' word divides those who refuse and reject it, those who receive it and keep it become one. Those alienated from Jesus become alienated from one another, "So there was a division in the crowd because of him" (7:43 NRSV). Jesus' opponents, the Pharisees, are divided because of him (9:16), as are the Judeans generally (10:19). But those at one with Jesus are at one with one another. This is the unity of love.

Jesus concludes his prayer with a plea that the love that the disciples have among themselves would be the same love that the Father has had for him. Jesus prays that the very love of God would be the love that they have for each other. His last bequest is that their love for each other would be divine.

SIX

A King of Shreds and Patches

"I'm going to die for the people because I'm going to live
for the people."[1]
—Fred Hampton, Chicago Black Panther Party
leader assassinated by Chicago police
December 4, 1969

The plot to kill Jesus is hatched in reaction to the groundswell of Jesus'
Judean acclaim following the resurrection of Lazarus: the plot even includes the
murder of Lazarus as well. Jesus' popularity as a political problem: the narrative
highlights the political logic of Jesus' arrest as a genuine oracle in the mouth of
the high priest. The "death that he was to die" will be as a consequence of Jesus'
exaltation, his having become a *nasi* in Jerusalem.

In John 12:42 the Pharisees bring their hostile influence to bear in the de-
liberations of the Jerusalem leaders, putting pressure on those who might be
positively disposed toward Jesus. The Jerusalem Pharisees are accessories to the
conspiracy against Jesus. But throughout the Gospel, the Pharisees are distinguished from the real decision-makers in Jerusalem, the priestly establishment.
The chief priests, and they alone, plot Jesus' death. The only Pharisees in the
Passion narrative of the Gospel of John, Nicodemus and Joseph of Arimathea,
are friendly toward Jesus. And so even the Pharisees are divided in their assess-
ment of Jesus. But the priests are of one mind that Jesus must die. The plot to kill
Jesus in Jerusalem begins in earnest in response to his overwhelming popularity
resulting from the resurrection of Lazarus, whereas in the Synoptic tradition the

plot is inaugurated with Jesus' entry into Jerusalem. Both traditions are in agreement, however, that it is precisely the acclamation of the masses that leads to Jesus' arrest. And Pilate's execution of a popular Israelite prophet comports with what we know of the way Romans handled popular movements, the very existence of which they considered threats to the imperial order.

Roman repression of agrarian prophets and their followers in Palestine was vicious, and Josephus's accounts of that repression are instructive. Between 44 and 46 CE, the Judean prophet Theudas led a multitude to the banks of the Jordan, where he claimed that the river would part at his command and allow the people to cross safely to the other side (*Ant.* 20.97-98). The Roman procurator Cuspius Fadus launched a surprise attack on them with a large cavalry force, killing many and taking prisoner those who survived the slaughter. Theudas was decapitated and his head was brought to Jerusalem. An Egyptian prophet (*Ant.* 20.169-171 = *War* 2.261-263) led a massive crowd to the Mount of Olives. He promised that the city walls would fall at his command. The Roman governor Felix fell upon the crowd with cavalry and infantry, killed 400 of the Egyptian's followers, and took 200 prisoners. The Egyptian escaped with his life and disappeared. Between 60 and 62 CE, Governor Festus sent out a force of cavalry and infantry to destroy a crowd that had followed an unnamed prophet into the Judean wilderness. The prophet and his followers were massacred (*Ant.* 20.188). And at the outbreak of hostilities in Jerusalem in the summer of 70, an unnamed prophet had collected over six thousand followers—many women and children—to await "signs of their liberation" (*War* 6.283-285). Roman soldiers set the Temple ablaze and slaughtered those who fled the flames.

The Jerusalem priests would tar Jesus with the brush of sedition. After his arrest, Jesus is led bound to the priest Annas, who in turn remanded him to the high priest Caiaphas, who finally handed him over to Pilate. Jesus was neither condemned nor sentenced before his appearance in the Praetorium. Pilate condemns Jesus only after the Jerusalem authorities make it clear that Jesus has popular support and is accused of a crime that is not merely an offense against arcane Judean sensibilities but a violation of the Roman order. It is Jesus' pretension to kingship that causes Pilate to condemn him to be crucified as "king of the Judeans."

We know of no crucifixions in Roman Palestine for which the Romans were not responsible. In the legislation of the Temple Scroll at Qumran (11QTemple 64:6-13) and in later rabbinic traditions about the death of Jesus (see, e.g., *b. Sanh.* 43a), the public suspension of the criminal's body is informed by Deut 21:23. This law commands that the felon's already dead body be hanged, presumably after having been stoned, as a sign of dishonor and a warning to the community. Apparently the ancient Israelites hanged those they executed to dishonor them. The Romans, however, hanged those they dishonored to execute them. Crucifixion was a practice perfected—if we may use that term—by the Romans, to which they lent their knack for technical precision and bloodthirsty brutality. In the first century of the Common Era, only the Roman occupation in Palestine would or could exact crucifixion as a capital punishment on disobedient slaves and rebellious provincials.

To crucify someone is to publicly torture him to death by stripping him naked, impaling him with iron nails on a crude wooden gibbet. The act of public execution in the narrative is encompassed in one simple phrase, "Jesus was crucified" (19:20 NRSV): the audience is expected to know what that means. That Jesus was nailed to a wooden cross and was then hoisted aloft amid cries of agony were gruesome details left unmentioned because they were so well and widely known.

Such an agonizing, ignominious death is many things. But it is not exaltation. Thus the phrase "lifting up" in John 3:14; 8:28; 12:31-32, referring to the exaltation of "the son of man," does not appear anywhere in the account of the crucifixion. After Jesus' claim that his exaltation—his being "lifted up from the earth"—would draw everyone to him, the narrator explains, "he said this signifying the kind of death he would die" (12:33). Traditionally the "lifting up" has been interpreted as Jesus' crucifixion, "the kind of death he would die." But nowhere in the entire narrative is the verb *hypsothenai*, "to be raised up," the verb the narrative consistently uses to speak of Jesus' exaltation, used to speak of Jesus' crucifixion. Much of traditional Christian theology has understood the crucifixion as exaltation. But this is a horrid oxymoron. By no stretch of the most perverse imagination could crucifixion have been understood this way anywhere in the Roman Empire in the first century of the Common Era.

The accounts of conflict and evasive maneuvers, coupled with the events of the crucifixion and resurrection of Jesus, together are elements of a complex "wisdom tale." The wisdom tale is "a story in which the protagonist is threatened with trial or ordeal but later is rescued, vindicated, and restored to power, while his or her opponents are made to suffer for their wrongdoing."[2] We find such narratives in the stories of Joseph (Gen 37-42), Ahikar, Mordecai's story in the book of Esther; Daniel 3 and 6; Susanna, which shares themes with Wisdom of Solomon 2; 4–5; 2 Maccabees 7; and 3 Maccabees.[3] The wisdom tale is not a story of personified wisdom; it is the story of the wrongful death of a righteous person, a "child of wisdom." The wisdom tale is generally characterized by a conspiracy against the protagonist is launched by his opponents. The protagonist is accused and tried, and, in spite of the intervention of a helper who comes to his aid and an opportunity to evade punishment, he is condemned. After an ordeal, which serves as a test of the validity of the protagonist's claims, a protest of innocence, a statement or prayer of trust in God's power to intervene, the protagonist is rescued, exalted, and vindicated.[4] Later adaptations of the wisdom tale treat the problem of the protagonist's senseless, untimely death.[5]

The rescue of the protagonist is at the climax of the traditional wisdom tale.[6] The rescue, not the protagonist's endurance, is key, for the rescue testifies to the protagonist's innocence.[7] Jesus, of course, is not rescued. But the passion narrative's bold violation of genre is not without venerable precedent. The book of Daniel had pioneered in its revolutionary adaptation of the Israelite wisdom tradition: "many of them that sleep in the dust shall awake," and the wise "shall shine as the stars of the firmament" (Dan 12:2, 3). We encounter this fundamental adaptation in the wisdom tale recounted in the Wisdom of Solomon. For the author of the Wisdom of Solomon, the only justice for the murdered righteous is immortality.

> But the souls of the righteous are in the hand of God, and no torment will ever touch them. In the eyes of the foolish they seemed to have died, and their departure was thought to be a disaster, and their going from us to be their destruction; but they are at peace. For though in the sight of others they were punished, their hope is full of immortality. Having been disciplined a little, they will receive great good, because God tested them and found them worthy of himself. Like gold in the furnace he tried them, and like a sacrificial burnt offering he accepted them. (Wis 3:1-6)

The death of the just ones is "like a sacrificial burnt offering"—a similitude, not an identity. They are not offered as sacrifices, but are "like" sacrifices in their innocence. As such, they are acceptable to God. The language of the paschal lamb describes the sufferings of Jesus. But the absence of sacrificial terms in describing the death of Jesus in the narrative suggests that the point of these allusions is Jesus' righteous innocence, not his sacrificial death. The Wisdom of Solomon describes this innocence and the wrath and violence it inspires.

> Let us lie in wait for the righteous man, because he is inconvenient to us and opposes our actions; he reproaches us for sins against the law, and accuses us of sins against our training. He professes to have knowledge of God, and calls himself a child of the Lord.... Let us see if his words are true, and let us test what will happen at the end of his life; for if the righteous man is God's child, he will help him, and will deliver him from the hand of his adversaries. Let us test him with insult and torture, so that we may find out how gentle he is, and make trial of his forbearance. Let us condemn him to a shameful death, for, according to what he says, he will be protected. (Wis 2:12-13, 17-20)

This reads as a veritable plot summary of the Beloved Community's story of Jesus, in which Jesus is just such a "righteous man." He disputes with legal authorities about his healing on the Sabbath, and defends his actions by referring to the practices of God his father (5:2-18). It is in the context of this dispute that Judeans resolve to kill Jesus (5:18). The Sabbath controversy is revisited in 7:21-24, and again Jesus invokes the authority of Moses against the Law of Moses. The chief priests and the Pharisees respond with an abortive attempt to arrest Jesus (7:32). The priests protest Pilate's offer of clemency with appeal to "law" (19:7). Because "he reproaches us for sins against the law, and accuses us of sins against our training" (Wis 2:12 NRSV) and because "he calls himself child of the Lord" (2:13) "and boasts that God is his father" (2:16), the enemies of Jesus plot against him (2:12). These conflicts and claims then set the stage for the passion narrative in which, in the words of Wisdom of Solomon, Jesus is tested with insult and torture (2:19) and condemned "to a shameful death" (2:20).

The myth of the suffering righteous one informed the Gospel's use of Israelite Scriptures that Jesus traditions impressed into the service of making sense of Jesus' death. The disposition of Jesus' dead body is explained in John 19:36-37 as the fulfillment of Exod 12:46; Num 9:12; and Zech 12:10. Jesus' body has been pierced and his bones remain unbroken because these are the scriptural characteristics of an innocent victim. The point of these allusions is Jesus' righteous innocence, not his sacrificial death. That Jesus should be a sacrificial lamb offered up for Israel is the final solution of the high priest Caiaphas (John 11:49-53), and we are reminded of his murderous prophecy in 18:14. Only those who conspire against Jesus understand his death as a sacrifice, a heinous interpretation of his execution from the lips of the narrative's arch-villain.

The narrative also uses the language of the beloved, "first-born" or "only-begotten" son to describe the sufferings of Jesus. It is not the language of divine sacrifice, but as the metaphor of righteous innocence. Divine paternity is the focus of the vituperative argument between Jesus and his Judean interlocutors in chapter 8. Jesus performs another healing on the Sabbath in chapter 9, provoking more legal debate. In chapter 10 Jesus claims unity with the Father, a claim that provokes yet another attempt to destroy him (10:30-31). Thus the first half of the narrative is punctuated by acrimonious conflicts over the Law and claims of divine paternity that come together in the theology of suffering found in the Wisdom of Solomon.

In John 19:24, Jesus' tunic is gambled away as he dies in fulfillment of Psalm 22:18 (NRSV): "They divide my clothes among themselves, and for my clothing they cast lots." In the Septuagintal version of Psalm 22, the mention of the loss of clothes in v. 18 is preceded by 21:17: "The have dug holes in my hands and feet." This Davidic Psalm is adduced just after the announcement of the text of the titulus over the cross, "Jesus the Nazarean, the King of the Jews." The allusion in Ps 22 addresses the problem of a king who suffers the scorn and derision of his enemies while weakened and defenseless. The narrative makes reference to Jesus as king or Jesus' kingdom ten times in two chapters—18:33, 36 (3x), 37; 19:3, 12, 14, 15, and 21. The references are clustered around discourse and narrative related to Pontius Pilate: they verbally register the confrontation of Jesus, the *nasi* of Israel, with Pilate, "the ruler of this world." Though the high priests quibble about Jesus' royal pretensions, the people recognized Jesus' claims, and so did Pilate, who inflicted upon him punishment worthy of a rebel king. At the end of the Galilean picnic for the masses in chapter 6, a parenthesis explains that Jesus refused to be drafted to popular kingship. In chapter 18, Jesus himself disclaims the political pretensions of his kingdom in his evasive conversation with Pontius Pilate. Thus Jesus appears apolitical at the very points where he appears most political. At the same time, the narration protests too much: his signs, his anointing, and his execution mark him as "king of the Judeans."

The Man Who Died (20:1-18)

"Master!" She said. "Oh, we have wept for you! And will you come back to us?"

"What is finished is finished, and for me the end is past," he said. "The stream will run till no more rain fills it, then it will dry up. For me, that life is over."

"Will you give up on your triumph?" she said sadly.

"My triumph," he said, "is that I am not dead."

— D. H. Lawrence, *The Man Who Died*

The martyr tale, unlike the wisdom tale, emphasizes the martyr's suffering and faithful endurance.[8] A martyr requires dignity in death, a grand farewell; a noble testimony that can be accommodated by hemlock, by the sword, even by the rack. The cross, however, accommodated only a pathetic cry of anguish. And though the most fanciful of ancient Christian narrators might have placed pained eloquence in the mouth of Jesus like that of the martyrs of 4 Maccabees, the interpretation of Jesus' death as martyrdom was untenable. Any effort to rehabilitate Jesus as a martyr was impossible after the ignominy of the cross. The martyr is the fallen hero of a cause that ultimately triumphs. As narrative, the disgrace of the cross would not allow vindication through the rhetoric of martyrdom. As history, the lost cause of liberation denied to Jesus the martyr's crown.

"Apart from a few remarks that point ahead to it," notes Ernst Käsemann, "the passion comes into view in [the Gospel of] John only at the very end. One is tempted to regard it as being a mere postscript that had to be included because John could not ignore this tradition nor yet could he fit it organically into his work. His solution was to press features of Christ's victory upon the passion story."[9] But the wisdom tale of the suffering righteous person, modified as it is in the books of Daniel and the Wisdom of Solomon to accommodate the death of the protagonist, is the narrative framework for the story of Jesus from beginning to end. There is no passion account as such; there is only the account—the account of Jesus as the perversely persecuted, wrongfully condemned, and ultimately vindicated child of Wisdom. It is this broad pattern of Israelite tradition, this "script" in the apt coinage of Richard Horsley,[10] which informs the story of Jesus from beginning to end. And the sheer brutality of the crucifixion constrained his vindication to come after the cross, because no plausible vindication could be found in it. The post-resurrection appearances of Jesus in chapters 20 and 21 are the narrative scar tissue covering the multiple wounds of the crucifixion. Easter alone realizes the requisite vindication of Jesus.

The first witness to this vindication is Mary Magdalene. We may discern some editorial seams in the account of her encounter of the resurrected Jesus as we now have it. Here is not one *angelus interpres,* but two, who nevertheless do not interpret anything. Peter "went out" (20:3), the same phrase that describes Judas in chapter 13. The singular verb suggests that the presence of the other disciple is redactional. Or perhaps the narration emphasizes Peter's treachery by applying Judas's description to him alone. On the other hand, the Old Sinaitic Syriac omits "Magdalene" in vv. 1 and 18. The post-resurrection appearance to Mary Magdalene is the beginning of association of the name of Mary with the empty tomb. Syrian tradition claimed that the Mary at the sepulcher was the mother of Jesus. The name Mary thus becomes identified with Jesus' mother, who remains anonymous to the Beloved Community. This Syrian tradition may have wished Jesus to meet his mother in the garden, and not a woman who over the centuries was rumored to have been his first apostle, his last friend, and more.

The scene is awash in tears. Mortality is refracted. Mary stands at the tomb weeping. The verb "weeping" appears twice in v. 11, once as a present participle and once in the imperfect, in the present tense in v. 13 in the inquiry of the angels, and again in 15 in the same tense and the same inquiry, repeated verbatim by Jesus. At another sepulcher earlier in the story we saw the powerful alchemy of a woman's tears. There, at the tomb of Lazarus, they inaugurated a resurrection. So too tears inaugurate the resurrection here. Here in the garden, the tears of a kneeling, anguished woman demand that Jesus deal with this crisis of mortality here as he had dealt with the other in Bethany—in person.

Mary comes to the garden alone. And after her brief, inconsequential attempt at conversation with Peter and the Beloved Disciple she remains alone. She speaks to the men but they do not answer her. They do not engage her. They engage in a foot race. Mary runs toward them, but they run toward the tomb. They do not find Jesus, and so go away. Mary states the fact of their common ignorance: "We do not know where they have put him." For the two disciples at the tomb, this ignorance is an indictment. Now, in a pitiful attempt to compensate for their desertion, they would rally in death to the man they deserted in life.

Mary comes to the garden empty-handed. She does not bear any of the paraphernalia of embalming. What was she hoping to find at the tomb? What would she do, what could she have done, had she found the corpse of the one she was looking for? Without companion, without implements, and without funereal accouterments, she seems strangely unprepared to find a dead body.

Mary comes to the garden while it is still dark—the cruel pall of death, cast over everything. Though the narrator assured us in the beginning that the light shines in the midst of the darkness and is not overcome by it (1:5), darkness is, for all that, an intransigent reality, perennially as real as the invincibility of light is true. With the dawn's early light, Mary encounters the risen Jesus. The correct rendering of 20:17 is not "Don't touch me" but "Stop touching me." Jesus insists that she stop embracing him because he wants to send her to his terrified comrades hiding in Jerusalem. "Mary Magdalene went and announced to the disciples, 'I have seen the Lord'; and she told them that he had said these things to her" (John 20:18 NRSV). As in the garden, the disciples give no reply.

Perhaps Mary met the silence from the wrong side of a bolted door. The narrative acknowledges that Easter proclamation coincided with Easter panic. The survivors of Jesus' crucifixion are huddled together in fear of the Judeans (20:19), in fulfillment of Jesus' prediction of their desertion (16:32). Narrative and discourse in the run-up to the first Easter are a dialectic of promises of safety and fits of terror. Jesus prays exclusively for the care of his followers at the end of their final meal (17:11); and at his arrest the narrator cites Scripture to the effect that none of Jesus' disciples are harmed or arraigned (see 18:8-9). Jesus assures Pilate that his servants do not fight (18:36). Yet violence attends Jesus' arrest (18:10). His disciples, put to flight, go underground.

Kierkegaard quipped that Christ comes to his followers through closed doors. Later Jesus, bearing the wounds of betrayal and desertion, comes to his barricaded disciples (20:19-24). Augustine observes, with rhetorical flourish, "And the disciple [i.e., Thomas] felt [him] and exclaimed, 'My Lord and my God.' Because he had touched a man, he confessed God."[11] But as we see in John 20:27-28, though Jesus invites Thomas to touch him, the text says nowhere that he actually does. The implication is to the contrary: Thomas has seen, he has believed, but he has not touched. Like Mary, he belatedly recognizes Jesus. But unlike Mary, he does not embrace him.

> . . . But the word has significance for those of us who wish to
> celebrate and share the certainty that the human condition is
> not a cesspool. Our writing is informed by a desire to make
> contact, so that readers may become involved with words
> that came to us from them, and that return to them as hope
> and prophecy.[1]

Jesus returns to Galilee to meet his disciples. It is clear, however, they do
not return to Galilee to meet him. The disciples for their part do not appear to
be seeking to meet Jesus anywhere, and do not appear to be expecting to meet
him anywhere. And whenever and wherever they do, they are surprised.

Julius Wellhausen has suggested that the miraculous meal of chapter 21 is
a parody of the miraculous meal of chapter 6, a travesty of the multiplication of
the loaves and fishes. The scenes are a study in contrasts, from the mountain
several hundred feet above to the lake several hundred feet below sea level. In
chapter 21 there are no mountains, no masses—and there is no movement. The
few remaining partisans of Jesus have literally gone fishing.

The scene of 21:1-14 is an ironic instance of superabundance, just as Peter's
promise of fealty is an ironic scene of apostolic commitment. Ironic, because the
audience knows that Peter has reneged on this commitment, and that the Beloved
Disciple lived to see him do so. It is Peter who suggests the fishing expedition
(21:3), a return to Galilean business as usual. There is a charcoal fire on the beach

(21:9) just there was a fire in the courtyard where Peter denied Jesus (18:18). Jesus inquires of Peter three times (21:15-19), just as Peter denied him three times. Jesus does not indicate that he is satisfied with Peter's affirmations. "If you love me," says Jesus, "you will lead my sheep out to pasture continually." Jesus has commanded Peter thrice to graze and pasture his flock. Not once does Peter say that he will do so.[2]

The first epilogue, 20:30-31, speaks of "what has been written," and why: "But these are written so that you may come to believe that Jesus is the Messiah, the Son of God, and that through believing you may have life in his name" (20:31 NRSV). The second epilogue treats the question of who has written. The disciple who has testified concerning the events and has written of them is "the beloved disciple" (21:20, 24). But there are other principals. "We," presumably the writer and his audience, know that the testimony of the Beloved Disciple is true (21:24), and "I," who offers an opinion in the last verse of the Gospel (21:25). Thus there are two writers, the Beloved Disciple and the opinionated "I," and two implied audiences: the one to which the Beloved Disciple wrote and the one to which the writer of 21:25 addresses his parting shot. Two epilogues, two writers, two audiences: the Gospel of John, as the First Epistle of John, is the fruit of a collaborative effort. A community read both works; but a community wrote both works as well.

And some of these anonymous writers were women, "chosen ladies" following the precedent of leadership set by the Elder's comradeship with the Elect Lady and her colleague. The influence of these women gave rise to an account of the life of Jesus that features women at several critical moments.[3] It is in Cana of Galilee, the site of Jesus' first "sign," that Jesus' anonymous mother speaks to him not as God's son but as her son. It is at her behest, his own hesitation notwithstanding, that he uses his powers to refresh the depleted wine at a wedding party. In Samaria, Jesus' interlocutor is a woman who tacitly engages the tortured sexual politics of the bitter schism between the Samaritans and the Judeans. After all, just before the First Judean War against Rome the synod of Hillelites and Shammaites agreed that "the daughters of Samaritans are menstruants from their cradle" (m. Niddah 4.1). Any pan-Israelite movement would have confronted the gendered ugliness of the Judeans' anti-Samaritan prejudice, and Samaritan women would have been especially keen to show Jesus affirming their embattled dignity in no uncertain terms.

The editorial contribution of women informed the inclusion of the story of the anonymous woman accused of adultery (7:53–8:11). Some Christians, including commentators and copyists, were uncomfortable with what struck some as Jesus' loose morality in this free-floating tale of adultery and absolution. John Calvin complained,

> It is not related that Christ simply absolved the woman, but that he let her go free. And this is not surprising, for He did not wish to undertake anything that did not belong to his office. Those who deduce from this that adultery should not be punished by death must, on the same reasoning, admit that inheritances should not be divided, since Christ refused to arbitrate between two brothers. Indeed every crime will be exempt from the penalties of law if the punishment of adultery is remitted, for the door will then be thrown open to every kind of treachery. . . .[4]

Moralists and text critics have tried to exclude the passage from the canon, and thereby from Christian sentiment and imagination. But their efforts have been in vain. The text has any one of several contexts in the manuscripts of the Bible, and so may belong properly to none of them. In some manuscript traditions the passage appears in the Gospel of Luke after 21:37-38 or after 24:50-53, both of which report Jesus' activities in the Temple. In other manuscripts it appears after John 21:25, an example of the "many other things Jesus did," or earlier in Temple scene after 7:36. The story contains the sole mention of scribes (3) and elders (9) in the Gospel of John. Jesus kneels down to write in the sand: perhaps one of the reasons the story circulated was to disconfirm, in the teeth of his literate opponents, accusation that Jesus is illiterate (7:15).[5] The story of the woman caught *in flagrante delecto* remains in the Bible, perhaps because, even if apocryphal, it is nonetheless true: in every age, hypocrisy is always but a stone's throw away.

The women who sat on that early, anonymous editorial board of the Beloved Community also ensured that Mary, the sister of Martha and Lazarus, would be remembered as anointing Jesus in anticipation of his royal reception in Jerusalem. Unlike the respective accounts of this event in Matthew and Mark, in the Gospel of John a woman anoints Jesus before, not after, his triumphal entry into Jerusalem. Even though Mark, and Matthew echoing Mark, records the anointing taking place after Jesus comes to Jerusalem, they agree with the Gospel of John that the anointing takes place not in Jerusalem but in the suburb of

Bethany. Matthew and Mark recount that Jesus is anointed in Bethany at the house of "Simon, a leper." But the Gospel of John is explicit that Martha is the party's hostess (12:2), and so it presumably takes place in her family's house. Matthew and Mark affirm that the woman's expensive gesture will be remembered wherever the gospel is preached: both Gospels, however, failed to mention her name. According to the Gospel of John, it is the other member of Jesus' beloved Bethanian family, Mary, who anoints Jesus at the party. And her name as well as her act are recorded for posterity.

And this is also why the story of Mary Magdalene, Peter, and the Other Disciple at the tomb is such an awkward, almost comical redaction, and why Peter and other disciples are not completely rehabilitated. The Beloved Disciple, however, adopted by Jesus' mother, is only man among the band of followers present at the crucifixion. He becomes the authoritative figure of the tradition but, like many of the women of the tradition, remains anonymous.

We may also expect the women of the Beloved Community to have favored its aversion to the Jerusalem Temple. For them, Israelite priesthood and its cult had always been a dead end. The Qumranites had made do without the Jerusalem Temple; after the war, the Rabbis would learn to make do without the Jerusalem priesthood. John the Baptist, with his one-note apocalyptic piety of ritual ablution, was already getting along quite well without both. And so the narrative of the Beloved Community places Jesus' debut in Peraea at the site of John's riverside appeal to all Israel. Jesus' appeal would be as grandiose in scope. But more aggressive: whereas Israel would come to John, Jesus would go to Israel in all its disparate territories.

The disciples of the Beloved Community looked back through the past to discover a love beyond all other loves. They found what the Elder had said, that is, the commandment that they had heard from the beginning. But the voice they heard was that of Jesus proclaiming a love supreme. The love of God was realized in Jesus and, the vicious catastrophe of the cross notwithstanding, that love had emerged victorious. Love trumped catastrophe. The events of the Passion could not compromise what the love of God had already accomplished in the Father's dispatch of his beloved son to his beloved world (John 3:16): thus Jesus declares victory before the events of the Passion (16:33). This is the consolation that love offers in the shadow of the cross, even on the eve of the death of hope. As the first Easter dawned, the community had failed (John 20). Its leaders had failed (John 21). Its projects, no matter how diminutive, failed: even a return to business as usual proved abortive (John 21). But Jesus returns to all these failures triumphant. Amid the darkness of the world, the light yet shines (John 1:5). Amid the failure of men, the love of God yet endures.

The Beloved Community tells us nothing of what happened to Jesus after breakfast in Galilee. The writing and writers of the Beloved Community, pass over the future past in silence. The death knell of any progressive movement sounds when the cult of personality springs up around its charismatic leader. The movement shifts into reverse all reflection on its practices and arrests the development of subsequent leadership. The future tends to be a denial of hope, all its eschatological rhetoric notwithstanding. The leader may be effectively mummified after death. The movement arrests its own development in an eternal, backward-looking present that identifies itself only with respect to the Great Man, or the Revolution, or the Founding Fathers. The dead leader becomes a myth, and the living leaders take on a *maiestas* that the dead leader would never have received, even if he had wanted it or had been willing to tolerate it. The future is dead on arrival. Its sense of the past corrupt and, consequently, its sense of the present bankrupt, the movement's self-understanding assumes a hostility to history as anything but apologia for the status quo ante: by appealing to what the leader did then it explains what we do now, as opposed to explaining what to do and how to do it based on what the leader did and how he did it.

Emphasis on the commandment—a commitment to the practices that make the movement move—saves the movement from becoming a cult of personality by challenging its partisans to be a community of practice that would keep faith with its founder through their solidarity with each other. This is the Elder's emphasis in his activity in the assembly and among the Chosen Ladies and those gathered around them. This is the emphasis that his letters laconically demand.

Having received their marching orders, the members of the Community do not look to Jesus to again take the field. There is no expectation that Jesus will return. Some Christians would insist that the Messiah is coming again—as if his first advent were not disappointing enough. With the aid of Christology, Christians are in denial about what Jews have learned with a wisdom borne of bitter experience: messiahs tend to be quite disappointing. The Beloved Community apparently did not aspire to such disappointment. Once was enough.

The editorial board that brought together the transcripts of the writer put forward the writer's theory of practice, so to speak. The editors did not put forward the person of the writer: that persona all but disappears behind his words. The writer in turn appeals to the practices of Jesus, whose actions reactivate an ancient ideal of love at least as old as Deuteronomy, the words of which were likely brought together in a written text after Israel had fallen apart.

That sensibility of the editorial board is manifest in the parenthetical commentary embedded in the narrative. Sometimes the words of Jesus and those of the narrator are elided in the text, as in John 3:31-36. The commentary intelligence, inseparable from the text as we now have it, is still discernible in parentheses and glosses, notices, to assist readers who may know the story but do not know the historical community in which it was first told:[6] Hebrew and Aramaic words (John 1:38, 41, 42; 4:25; 5:2; 9:7; 11:16; 19:13, 17; 20:16, 24; 21:2); Judean practices (2:6; 4:9; 18:28; 19:40), and claims for the fulfillment of Scripture (1:23; 2:17; 6:31; 7:38; 12:14-16; 18:9, 32; 19:24, 28, 36-37; 20:9). This commentary intelligence is not engaged with the Beloved Community. It is engaged with that community's text. The query in John 7:35, "Will he go to the Dispersion?" goes unanswered in the story, as does the delegation of "some Greeks" who have come to Jerusalem for the Passover (12:20-26). The narrative does not extend its scope beyond Palestine: Jesus did not go to the Diaspora. But his story did, laced with annotations provided by those who still shared both his language and his culture so that those who shared neither could share his story.

These parentheses are not the words of the Beloved Community. The glossators live in that community no more than an archaeologist lives in an excavation site, and for similar reasons. The story was only somewhat less alien to those who wrote the parentheses than it was to those for whom they were written. What they have written has the status of the apparatus of a text: its proximity to the words is measured in micrometers on the page but in years and in some instances centuries of human life. The great uncial codices Sinaiticus (א) from the fourth century and Codex Bezae (D) from the fifth century CE both lack the explanatory parenthesis of John 4:9, "Judeans do not share things in common with Samaritans." The parenthesis is emblematic: it is of much less importance to the text than it is to text criticism.

I intuit that other editorial features of the narrative, however, are the inscribed decisions of the editorial board. The ingenious, almost perverse exegesis of John 10:34-35 is not an intervention of the narrator, and so I would not include it under the rubric of alien commentary. Nor do I include under that rubric the pastiche of citations from Isaiah in John 12:39-41, which the narrator recalls not as what Isaiah wrote but what "Isaiah said." The narrator relates the spirit of the prophet here, not the letter. The distinction is important, because one of the developments that take place in the story's written form is a changing sensibility about writing and about what is written. In the fulfillment proof texts, the story of the Beloved Community has now become a written a text that calls for and calls to other texts. And from that moment on, all subsequent readers enter into communication with the Beloved Community as a link from the other end of what has devolved into a chain of literary representations.

Now that the writers are recounting the story in writing, they have committed the words of Jesus, and their own words, to narrative. Unlike the discourse of a letter or the concatenated musings of the writer in 1 John, narrative is not occasional. A written narrative begins to transcend the very contingency of communication—what happens to call words from speakers—and the evanescence of communication—the impermanence of the spoken word only partially captured in that changeable imagination of the past that we call memory.

All that is left is the words: the words of Jesus, the words of his several interlocutors, and finally, the words of the anonymous testators who have put forward a narrative that rests upon their testimony. "If the contemporary generation," writes Kierkegaard of these writers, "had left nothing behind them but theses words: 'We have believed that in such and such a year God appeared among us in the humble figure of a servant, that he lived and taught in our community, and finally died,' it would be more than enough."[7] Words written that we may believe, that we "may become involved with words that came to us from them," that the Love Supreme to which they bear witness may be for us prophecy and hope.

Abbreviations

ℵ	Codex Sinaiticus (01), fourth century
A	Codex Alexandrinus (02), fifth century
AB	Anchor Bible
ANRW	*Aufstieg und Niedergang der römischen Welt*
Ant.	Josephus, *Antiquities*
1 Apol.	Justin Martyr, *First Apologia*
B	Codex Vaticanus (03), fourth century
b.	Babylonian Talmud (*Bavli*)
b.	bar or ben (in Aramaic or Hebrew names)
BBET	Beiträge zur biblischen Exegese und Theologie
BJRL	*Bulletin of the John Rylands Library*
BJS	Brown Judaic Studies
BTB	*Biblical Theology Bulletin*
BZAW	Beihefte zur Zeitschrift für die alttestamentliche Wissenschaft
BZNW	Beihefte zur Zeitschrift für die neutestamentliche Wissenschaft
C	Codex Ephraimi (04), fifth century
CBQ	*Catholic Biblical Quarterly*
CD	Damascus Document
Cher.	Philo, *De cherubim* (On the Cherubim)
D	Codex Bezae (05), fifth century
Det.	Philo, *Quod deterius potiori insidari soleat* (That the Worse Attacks the Better)
EBib	Etudes bibliques

Erub.	ʿErubin
GCS	Die griechische christliche Schriftsteller der ersten Jahrhunderte
Gen. Rab.	*Genesis Rabbah*
Giṭ.	*Giṭṭin*
HTKNT	Herders theologischer Kommentar zum Neuen Testament
JAAR	*Journal of the American Academy of Religion*
JBL	*Journal of Biblical Literature*
JTS	*Journal of Theological Studies*
Kil.	*Kilʾayim*
LEC	Library of Early Christianity
LXX	Septuagint
m.	Mishnah
Maʿaś.	*Maʿaśerot*
Mos.	Philo, *De vita Mosis* (On the Life of Moses)
MT	Masoretic text
Mut.	Philo, *De mutatione nominum* (On the Change of Names)
NovT	*Novum Testamentum*
NPNF	Nicene and Post-Nicene Fathers
NTS	*New Testament Studies*
OBT	Overtures to Biblical Theology
Opif.	Philo, *De opificio mundi* (On the Creation of the World)
P	Codex Porphyrianus (025), ninth century
𝔓74	Papyrus 74 (Bodmer XVII), seventh century
Pesiq. Rab.	*Pesiqta Rabbati*
PL	J.-P. Migne, editor, *Patrologiae cursus completus: Series latina*. 218 vols. Paris: Garnier, 1844–64
Praep. evang.	Eusebius, *Praeparatio evangelica* (Preparation of the Gospel)
Prob.	Philo, *Quod omnis probus liber sit* (That Every Good Person Is Free)
Ps. Sol.	*Psalms of Solomon*
1QH	Hymn Scroll (*Hodayoth*)
1QS	Community Rule (*Serek ha-Yaḥad*)
1QSa	Rule of the Congregation (Appendix a to 1QS)
4QpNah	Nahum Pesher (4Q169)
R.	rabbi

Rom.	Ignatius, *To the Romans*
Sac.	Philo, *De sacrificiis Abelis et Caini* (On the Sacrifices of Abel and Cain)
Som.	Philo, *De somniis* (On Dreams)
Tem.	*Temurah*
Tim.	Plato, *Timaeus*
W	Freer Codex (032), fourth to fifth century
War	Josephus, *The Jewish War*
y.	Jerusalem Talmud (*Yerushalmi*)

Notes

Acknowledgments

1. Elisabeth Schüssler Fiorenza, *In Memory of Her* (New York: Crossroads, 1989), 68–95, 105–159, and 323–34.

2. Elisabeth Schüssler Fiorenza, "The Quest for the Johannine School: The Book of Revelation and the Fourth Gospel," in *The Book of Revelation: Justice and Judgment*, 2d ed. (Minneapolis: Fortress Press, 1998), 85–113.

3. Obery M. Hendricks Jr., "A Discourse of Domination: A Socio-Rhetorical Study of the Use of *Ioudaios* in the Fourth Gospel" (Princeton University, 1995).

4. Daniel Boyarin, "The *Ioudaioi* in John and the Prehistory of 'Judaism'," in *Pauline Conversations in Context: Essays in Honor of Calvin Roetzel*, edited by Janice Capel Anderson, Philip Sellew, and Claudia Setzer, Journal for the Study of the New Testament Supplement Series 221 (Sheffield: Sheffield Academic, 2002), 216–39.

Prologue

1. F. F. Bruce, "St. John at Ephesus," *BJRL* 60 (1977–78) 339–61, see 341–42.

2. Michel Foucault, "What Is an Author?" in *Language, Counter-Memory, Practice*, Donald F. Bouchard, ed. (Ithaca, New York: Cornell Univ. Press, 1977), 107.

3. Foucault, "What Is an Author?" 107.

4. Roland Barthes, "The Death of the Author," *Image/Music/Text*, trans. Stephen Heath (London: Hill and Wang, 1977), 225.

5. Foucault, "What Is an Author?" 118.

6. Jo Anne Marie Terrell, *"Power in the Blood"?: The Cross in the African American Experience* (Maryknoll, N.Y.: Orbis, 1998), 123.

7. This eloquent phrase is from the sermon of Forrest Church, "The Fear of Jesus," preached Easter Sunday April 11, 2004. www.allsoulsnyc.org/publications/sermons/fcsermons/easter-2004.html.

1. Root Conflict

1. In *II Epistolam Joannis* (Migne, PL col. 120).

2. *Sed nunc generalis Ecclesiae consensus quod has quoque Epistolas Joannes apostolus scripterit* (In *II Epistolam Joannis*, col. 119).

3. Martin S. Jaffee, "A Rabbinic Ontology of the Written and Spoken Word: On Discipleship, Transformative Knowledge, and the Living Texts of the Oral Torah," *JAAR* 65 (1997) 528; he cites as an example *b. Erub.* 54b.

4. Jaffee, "Rabbinic Ontology," 537.

5. H. L. Strack and Günter Stemberger, *Introduction to the Talmud and Midrash*, 2d ed., trans. and ed. Markus Bockmuehl (Minneapolis: Fortress Press, 1996), 31–37. In Jaffee, "Rabbinic Ontology," 528.

6. *y. Ma'aś.* 2:4, 49d; *y. Kil.* 1:1, 27a.

7. Jaffee, "Rabbinic Ontology," 537.

8. *b. Tem.* 14b; cf. *b. Giṭ.* 60b; *y. Pe'ah* 2:6, 17a, and parallels; cited in Jaffee, "Rabbinic Ontology," 536.

9. Fredrick Jameson, *The Political Unconscious: Narrative as a Socially Symbolic Act* (London: Methuen, 1981).

10. Eduardo Galeano, "In Defense of the Word," in *We Say No: Chronicles 1963–1991*, trans. Mark Fried et al. (New York: Norton, 1992), 139.

11. In Otto Stählin, ed., *Clemens Alexandrinus*, vol. 3 (Berlin: Akademie, 1970), 215.

12. J. A. Cramer, *Catena in Epistolas Catholicas* (Oxford: E Typographeo academico, 1840), 146–47. The text of Sinaiticus reads "the likewise elect church in Babylon."

13. Cheryl Townsend Gilkes, "The Virtues of Brotherhood and Sisterhood: African American Fraternal Organizations and Their Bibles," in *African Americans and the Bible: Sacred Texts and Social Textures*, ed. Vincent L. Wimbush (New York: Continuum, 2000), 399.

2. Disciples of the Beloved Community

1. In Otto Stählin, ed., *Clemens Alexandrinus*, vol. 3, (Berlin: Akademie, 1970), 210.

2. *Quoniam abrupta est et confusa oratio.* In August Tholuck, ed., *Ioannis Calvini in Novum Testamentum Commentarii,* vol. 7 (Berlin: Gustavus Eichler, 1834), 276.

3. *Verum nihil horum continua serie facit. Nam sparsim docendo et exhortando varius est.* In ibid., 275.

4. See Georg Strecker, *The Johannine Letters,* trans. Linda M. Maloney, Hermeneia (Minneapolis: Fortress Press, 1996), 17.

5. M.-E. Boismard, "The First Epistle of John and the Writings of Qumran," in *John and Qumran,* ed. James H. Charlesworth (London: Chapman, 1972), 156.

6. Ibid., 159.

7. Ibid.

8. Ibid., 160.

9. Spicq, *Agapè,* 302.

10. Boismard, "First Epistle," 159.

11. Ibid., 160.

12. Ibid., 160–61.

13. *Prob.* 85-86.

14. John Dominic Crossan, *The Birth of Christianity* (San Francisco: HarperSanFrancisco, 1998), 445.

15. Boismard, "First Epistle," 160.

16. See Spicq, *Agapè,* 261, note 6.

17. See Wescott, *Epistles of Saint John,* 12 on use of noun with *echo* plus the noun instead of the verb.

18. Paul Ramsey, *Nine Modern Moralists* (Englewood Cliffs, N.J.: Prentice-Hall, 1962), 153–54.

19. Boismard, "First Epistle," 160.

20. See Strecker, *Letters,* 32 n. 30.

21. Anders Nygren, *Agape and Eros: A Study of the Christian Idea of Love,* trans. A. G. Herbert (New York: Macmillan, 1932), 110.

22. In v. 12, however, important minuscules have preserved the proper reading: the parallelism of 2:12–14 calls for *paidia,* and not *teknia.* The latter reading comes into the manuscript tradition early under the influence of the other appearances of *teknia* in the text. The minuscule 630 suggests that 2:12 echoes the direct address in 2:1, for this minuscule reads the same "my little children," *teknia mou,* of 2:1.

23. *Patres non aetate, sed sapientia majores ac matures appellat* (Col. 91).

24. In Strecker, *Letters,* 56.

25. E. Franklin Frazier, *The Negro Church in America* (New York: Schocken, 1966), 1.

26. Spicq, *Agapè*, 250.

27. In Stählin, ed., *Clemens Alexandrinus*, 31:214.

28. See Strecker, *Letters*, 237.

29. Everywhere but Dan 9:26 and Sir 38:30.

30. See Pheme Perkins, "Koinonia in 1 John 1:3–7: The Social Context of Division in the Johannine Letters," *CBQ* 45 (1983) 631–41, especially 639.

31. The second person plural pronoun at the beginning of v.27 is emphatic, unusual, and confusing to the manuscript tradition, setting off a chain reaction of variants. Once again Alexandrinus is a faithful guide, including the omission of the superfluous *kai* that precedes the last clause.

32. See Strecker, *Letters*, 84 nn. 33–37.

33. See Schnackenburg, *Epistles*, 179, n. 191; Brown, *Epistles*, 442; Strecker, *Letters*, 109.

34. *Derek 'Erets* 10.

35. Ludwig Wittgenstein, *Tractatus Logico-Philosophicus*, trans. D. F. Pears and B. F. McGuiness (New York: Humanities, 1963), 151.

36. Ibid., 151. Italics in the original.

37. Ibid.

38. Wittgenstein, *Tractatus*, 51.

39. Charles Long, "Silence and Signification," in *Significations: Signs, Symbols, and Images in the Interpretation of Religion* (Philadelphia: Fortress Press, 1986), 60–61.

40. Long, "Silence and Signification," 61.

41. Anders Nygren, *Agape and Eros: A Study of the Christian Idea of Love*, trans. A. G. Herbert (New York: Macmillan, 1932), 113–14.

42. Nygren, *Agape and Eros*, 115.

43. C. Spicq, *Agapè, Prolégomènes à une étude de théologie néo-testamentaire*, Studia Hellenistica 10 (Leiden: Brill, 1955), 89. Quoted in William L. Moran, "The Ancient Near Eastern Background of the Love of God in Deuteronomy," *CBQ* 25 (1963), 77.

44. Ibid.

45. Moran, "Background," 77–78.

46. Ibid., 78.

47. Ibid., 82.

48. Ibid., 79.

49. Enrique Dussel, from *Ethics and Community*, translated by Robert Barr (Maryknoll, N.Y.: Orbis, 1988), in *The Postmodern Bible Reader*, David Jobling, Tina Pippin, and Ronald Schleifer, eds. (Oxford: Blackwell, 2001), 304.

50. "...propose une application telle banale: secourir les necessiteux," Spicq, *Agape*, 261.

51. *Ecce unde incipit caritas* . . . *Si enim superflua non potes dare fratri tuo, animam tuam potes ponere pro fratre?* (Migne, PL 351:2018).

52. NPNF 14:96.

53. Spicq, *Agape*, 258. "Toute l'economie chrétienne est ainsi centrée sur la charité: Au sein de l'Église—car il s'agit toujours d'aimer *ses frères*—vivre, c'est aimer."

54. Spicq, *Agapè*, 279.

55. Among the most compelling of many examples that could be adduced, see Mic 4:4 and Isa 58.

56. Cramer, *Catena*, 128.

57. Reinhold Niebuhr, *An Interpretation of Christian Ethics* (New York: Meridian, 1958), 164.

58. "Though the variant reading ['every spirit that destroys Jesus'] has not been preserved in the text of any extant Greek manuscript, its originality over against the common reading . . . is proven not only by the fact that Irenaeus, Clement of Alexandria, Origen, and Tertullian have it, but especially by the fact that the Vulgate reads *solvit Jesum*. The difficulty the ancient Fathers had to make sense of this awkward phrase . . . point to the originality of this unique expression." Otto A. Piper, "I John and the Didache of the Primitive Church," *JBL* 66 (1947) 443. Piper proposes a Semitic *Vorlage* for the variant. The Greek verb, *luein*, usually has the sense "to loose, to destroy," but here has the sense "to disobey, transgress." This is exactly the sense it has in John 5:18, "he was violating (*eluen*) the Sabbath."

59. Cramer, *Catena*, 131.

60. The words "to be," "to listen," "world," and "God" are the lexical links between this treatment and the foregoing. The plural object pronoun in 4:4 and the absence of a consequential particle such as "because, for," *hoti* or "and so," *de* at the beginning of the verse suggest that something is missing. Perhaps the two discourses, originally separate with the antecedent of "them," *autous*, intervening, have been joined due to lexical affinities.

61. In 5:13–21, "that the life we have is eternal," the word "eternal" is a predicate adjective. Contrast the construction in 1:2, "eternal life," in which the adjective is attributive. The protasis, "if we ask," and the apodosis, "[then] he hears us," comprise verse 5:14. We may follow the minority witnesses and omit the "not" in 17b. The sense is "Every (or 'all') injustice is sin, that is, it is sin unto death."

62. Nygren, *Agape*, 108.

63. I follow here Hanna Arendt's treatment in her 1929 dissertation on Augustine and love, *Love and Saint Augustine*, Joanna Vecchiarelli Scott and Judith Chelius Stark, eds. (Chicago: Univ. of Chicago Press, 1996).

64. Paul Tillich, *Dynamics of Faith* (New York: Harper, 1957), 112.

65. Ibid., 113.

66. Ibid., 115.

67. Paul Tillich, *Systematic Theology* (Chicago: Univ. of Chicago Press, 1951–63), 1.136.

68. Strecker, *Letters*, 172. The clauses in vv. 20–21 are a syntactical challenge, as the variegated manuscript witnesses attest. We must read *ean* as *an* at the beginning of v. 21 and v. 22. Indeed vv. 20–22 repeat the pattern of sentences signifying contingency, introduced by the particle *an* and by *hoti,* the latter to be distinguished from *ho ti,* at the end of the clause in 20a.

69. On King's thought and his intellectual influences in the academy, I have been aided here by the treatment of John Ansbro, *Martin Luther King, Jr.: Non-Violent Strategies and Tactics for Social Change* (Lanham, Md.: Madison, 2000).

70. Martin Luther King Jr., "A Comparison of the Conception of God in the Thinking of Paul Tillich and Henry Nelson Wieman." Ph.D. dissertation in Systematic Theology, Boston University, 1955, 149.

71. King, "A Comparison," 147.

72. Walter Fluker, "They Looked for a City: A Comparison of the Ideal of Community in Howard Thurman and Martin Luther King, Jr.," *The Drew Gateway* 61 (Fall 1991), 10.

73. King, *Where Do We Go From Here: Chaos or Community?* (New York: Harper & Row, 1967), excerpted in James Melvin Washington, *A Testament of Hope: The Essential Writings of Martin Luther King, Jr.* (San Francisco: Harper & Row, 1986), 632.

74. In Washington, *Testament*, 16.

75. "The Most Durable Power," *Christian Century* 74 (5 June 1957) 10–11, in Washington, *Testament*, 708.

76. *Et mundus omnis in maligno constitutus est non creatura, sed saeculares hominess et secundum concupiscentias viventes.* In Stählin, ed., *Clemens Alexandrinus*, 3:214.

77. Thus we must read 5:20a, along with the minority witnesses, as "the true God," because 5:20b, "in him," requires the antecedent noun "God." The substantive adjective "the true" as the antecedent here will not do. The *kai* in 5:20a is epexegetical: "the true God, that is, eternal life." Just as God is love, so God is eternal life.

78. Bedae Venerabilis opp. Pars. II sec. I—*Exegetica Genuina*, Migne, PL 74, vol. 4, col. 120: *doctrinis haereticorum, que perpetuam ducunt ad mortem.*

79. *philargyria, quae est simulacrorum servitus.*

80. Hartmut Günther and Ernst Volk, eds., *D. Martin Luthers Epistel-Auslegung*, vol. 5 (Göttingen: Vandenhoek & Rupecht, 1983), 358.

81. A. Tholuck, ed., *Ioannis Calvini in Novum Testamentum Commentarii*, vol. 7 (Berlin: Eichler, 1834),340.

82. Rudolf Bultmann, *The Johannine Epistles*, trans. R. Phillip O'Hara with Lane C. McGaughy and Robert Funk, Hermeneia (Philadelphia: Fortress Press, 1973), 2.

83. Again we follow the reading of A, which makes clearer the implicit contrast between the authentic God of Jesus Christ in 5:20 and the inauthentic deity of the idols in 5:21. The parallelism of 5:20 with 5:21 commends Alexandrinus's reading of *theon*, just as the parallelism in 2:12 supports the reading of *paidia*.

84. 1QS 2.11–17. See Boismard, "First Epistle," 161.

85. Boismard, "First Epistle," 161.

86. Ibid.

87. Elaine Scarry, "The Interior Structure of Made Objects," in Jobling, et al., eds., *The Postmodern Bible Reader*, 280–81.

88. Jack Miles, *Christ: A Crisis in the Life of God* (New York: Vintage, 2001), 275.

89. Ibid., 276.

90. Julia Kristeva, "Reading the Bible," in *The Postmodern Bible Reader*, 97.

3. The Spiritual Gospel

1. Jo Anne Marie Terrell, *"Power in the Blood"?: The Cross in the African American Experience* (Maryknoll, N.Y.: Orbis, 1998), 125.

2. See especially Exod 33:17–34:7.

3. John A. T. Robinson, "The Use of the Gospel of John for Christology Today," in Barnabas Lindars and Stephen Smalley, eds., *Christ and the Spirit in the New Testament* (Cambridge: Cambridge Univ. Press, 1973), 70.

4. Mogens Stiller Kjaärgaard, *Metaphor and Parable*, Acta theologica Danica 20 (Leiden: Brill, 1986), 106.

5. Dewey, "Paroimai," 92.

4. In Those Parts

1. B. Oded, "Observation on Methods of Assyrian Rule in Transjordania After the Palestinian Campaign of Tiglath-Pileser III," *Journal of Near Eastern Studies* 29 (1970) 183; quoted in Younger, "Deportation," 213.

2. Younger, "Deportation," 227.

3. See Sean Freyne, "The Geography of Restoration: Galilee-Jerusalem Relations in Early Jewish and Christian Experience," *NTS* 47 (2001) 309–10.

4. See Brown, *John*, 105.

5. Prior, *Bible and Colonialism*, 223.

6. In Sargon's *Annals*, 123a. In Andreas Fuchs, *Die Inschriften Sargons II aus Khorsabad* (Göttingen: Cuvillier, 1994), 110. Quoted in K. Lawson Younger, Jr., "The Deportation of the Israelites," *JBL* 117 (1998) 226.

7. Jonathan A. Goldstein, "Jewish Acceptance and Rejection of Hellenism," in E. P. Sanders, ed., *Jewish and Christian Self-Definition* (Philadelphia: Fortress Press, 1981), 77.

8. See Robert Carroll, "The Myth of the Empty Land," *Semeia* 59 (1992) 81.

9. Thomas L. Thompson, *Early History of the Israelite People from the Written and Archaeological Sources*, Studies in the History of the Ancient Near East 4 (Leiden: Brill, 1992), 418.

10. Aitken, "At the Well," 345.

11. Haenchen, *The Gospel of John*, 2.222.

12. The genitive absolute in the Greek is causative.

13. Cory, "Wisdom's Rescue," 113.

14. See J. L. Rubenstein, *The History of Sukkot in the Second Temple and Rabbinic Periods*, BJS 302 (Atlanta: Scholars, 1995), 117–52.

15. Rubenstein, *History of Sukkot*, 148, n. 168.

16. Joel Marcus has proposed Isa 12:3 as the source text. Joel Marcus, "Rivers of Living Water from Jesus' Belly" (John 7:38)," *JBL* 1172 (1998) 329 n. 5.

5. Love *in extremis*

1. See Henri Nouwen, *Lifesigns: Intimacy, Fecundity, and Ecstasy in Christian Perspective* (Garden City, N.Y.: Doubleday, 1986).

2. Reinhold Niebuhr, *An Interpretation of Christian Ethics* (New York: Harper, 1935), 220.

6. A King of Shreds and Patches

1. Quoted in Mike Gray, *The Murder of Fred Hampton*, documentary (Hollywood: VDI [distributor], 1971).

2. Catherine Cory, "Wisdom's Rescue: A New Reading of the Tabernacle Discourse," *JBL* 1161 (1997) 95–116. Catherine Cory has described the Tabernacles discourse (John 7:1–8:59) as "a unique Johannine innovation, a story about Wisdom's 'rescue' from the enemies' hands" (95).

3. See George Nickelsburg, *Resurrection, Immortality, and Eternal Life in Intertestamental Judaism* (Cambridge: Harvard Univ. Press, 1972) 56–57.

4. Cory, "Wisdom's Rescue," 95–96. Optional features are an expression of amazement from the protagonist's opponents, a confession by the opponents (usually including an acknowledgement of their wrongful accusations), the condemnation of the protagonist's opponents, and the punishment of the opponents.

5. Ibid., 107.

6. Ibid., 106.

7. Ibid., 98.

8. Ibid., 98.

9. Ernst Käsemann, *The Testament of Jesus*, trans. Gerhard Krodel (Philadelphia: Fortress Press, 1966), 7.

10. Richard Horsley, *Hearing the Whole Story: The Politics of Plot in Mark's Gospel* (Louisville: Westminster John Knox, 2001), 235.

11. ... *et palpavit ille discipulus et exclamavit, Dominus meus et Deus meus. Quia tetigit hominem, confessus est Deum.* In Epistolam Joannis, Migne, PL 35, col. 1980.

7. Epilogues

1. Galeano, "In Defense of the Word," in *We Say No*, 140.

2. Note the verbs. I am indebted to Krister Stendahl for pointing out to me that, properly speaking, sheep are not fed: they are let out to pasture and led to grazing lands where they may feed themselves.

3. Elisabeth Schüssler Fiorenza, *In Memory of Her* (New York: Crossroads, 1989), 323–34.

4. John Calvin, *The Gospel According to Saint John*, ed. D. W. Torrance and T. F. Torrance, trans. T. H. L. Parker (Grand Rapids: Eerdmans, 1959), 209.

5. Walter Baur has conjectured that an early polemic directed against Jesus claimed that he did not know how to read. Walter Baur, *Das Johannesevangelium*, HNT 6 (Tubingen: Mohr/Siebeck, 1933), 109.

6. For the classifications of parentheses as identified by various scholars of the Gospel of John, see Gilbert van Belle, *Les parenthèses dans l'Évangile de Jean: Aperçu historique et classification texte grec de Jean* (Leuven: Leuven Univ. Press, 1985), 106–12, to which this treatment is indebted.

7. Søren Kierkegaard, *Philosophical Fragments*, tr. David F. Swenson (Princeton: Princeton Univ. Press, 1936), 87.

Bibliography

Aitken, Ellen. "At the Well of Living Water: Jacob Traditions in John 4." In *The Interpretation of Scripture in Early Judaism and Christianity*, edited by Craig A. Evans. Studies in Scripture in Early Judaism and Christianity 7. Sheffield: Sheffield Academic, 2000.

Ansbro, John. *Martin Luther King, Jr.: Non-Violent Strategies and Tactics for Social Change*. Lanham, Md.: Madison, 2000.

Arendt, Hannah. *Love and Saint Augustine*. Edited by Joanna Vecchiarelli Scott and Judith Chelius Stark. Chicago: Univ. of Chicago Press, 1996.

Ashton, John. *Understanding the Fourth Gospel*. Oxford: Clarendon, 1991.

Barthes, Roland. "The Death of the Author." In *Image/Music/Text*. Trans. Stephen Heath. London: Hill and Wang, 1977.

Boismard, M.-E. "The First Epistle of John and the Writings of Qumran." In *John and Qumran*, ed. James H. Charlesworth, 156–65. London: Chapman, 1972.

Brown, Raymond E. *The Community of the Beloved Disciple*. New York: Paulist, 1979.

―――. *The Epistles of John*. AB 30. Garden City, N.Y.: Doubleday, 1982.

―――. *The Gospel of John*. 2 vols. AB 29, 29A. Garden City, N.Y.: Doubleday, 1966, 1970.

Bruce, F. F. "St. John at Ephesus." *BJRL* 60 (1977–78) 339–61.

Bultmann, Rudolf. *The Johannine Epistles*. Translated by R. Philip O'Hara with Lane C. McGaughy and Robert Funk. Hermeneia. Philadelphia: Fortress Press, 1973.

―――. *Theology of the New Testament*. 2 vols. Translated by Kendrick Grobel. New York: Scribner, 1955.

Burney, C. F. *The Aramaic Origins of the Fourth Gospel*. Oxford: Clarendon, 1922.

Calvin, John. *The Gospel According to Saint John*. Edited by D. W. Torrance and T. F. Torrance. Translated by T. H. L. Parker. Grand Rapids: Eerdmans, 1959.

Carroll, Robert. "The Myth of the Empty Land." *Semeia* 59 (1992) 79–93.

Conzelmann, Hans. "Was von Anfang war." In *Neutestamentliche Studien für Rudolf Bultmann*, edited by Walther Eltester, 194–201. BZNW 21. Berlin: Töpelmann, 1957.

Cory, Catherine. "Wisdom's Rescue: A New Reading of the Tabernacles Discourse (John 7:1–8:59)." *JBL* 116 (1997) 95–116.

Cramer, J. A. *Catena in Epistolas Catholicas: Accesserunt Oecumenii et Arethae Commentarii in Apocalypsin.* Oxford: E Typographeo academico, 1840.

Crossan, John Dominic. *The Birth of Christianity: Discovering What Happened in the Years Immediately after the Execution of Jesus.* San Francisco: HarperSanFrancisco, 1998.

Dewey, Kim. "*Paroimia* in the Gospel of John." *Semeia* 17 (1980) 81–99.

Di Vito, Robert A. "Old Testament Anthropology and the Construction of Personal Identity." *CBQ* 61 (1999) 217–38.

Dodd, C. H. *Historical Tradition in the Fourth Gospel.* Cambridge: Cambridge Univ. Press, 1963.

———. *The Interpretation of the Fourth Gospel.* Cambridge: Cambridge Univ. Press, 1953.

Dussel, Enrique. *Ethics and Community.* Translated by Robert R. Barr. Maryknoll, N.Y.: Orbis, 1988.

Fanon, Frantz. *Black Skin, White Masks.* Translated by Charles Lam Markmann. New York: Grove, 1967.

Feuillet, André. "The Structure of First John: Comparison with the Fourth Gospel." *BTB* 3 (1973) 194–216.

Fitzmyer, Joseph A. "Crucifixion in Ancient Palestine, Qumran Literature, and the New Testament." *CBQ* 40 (1978) 493–513.

Foucault, Michel. "What Is an Author?" In *Language, Counter-Memory, Practice*, 124–42. Translated by Donald F. Bouchard and Sherry Simon. Ithaca, N.Y.: Cornell Univ. Press, 1977.

Fuchs, Andreas. *Die Inschriften Sargons II aus Khorsabad.* Göttingen: Cuvillier, 1994.

Galeano, Eduardo. *We Say No: Chronicles 1963–1991.* Translated by Mark Fried et al. New York: Norton, 1992.

Gilkes, Cheryl Townsend. "The Virtues of Brotherhood and Sisterhood: African American Fraternal Organizations and Their Bibles." In *African Americans and the Bible: Sacred Texts and Social Textures*, edited by Vincent L. Wimbush. New York: Continuum, 2000.

Goldstein, Jonathan A. "Jewish Acceptance and Rejection of Hellenism." In *Jewish and Christian Self-Definition*, edited by E. P. Sanders, vol. 2, 64–87 Philadelphia: Fortress Press, 1981.

Haenchen, Ernst. *The Gospel of John.* 2 vols. Translated by Robert W. Funk. Hermeneia. Philadelphia: Fortress Press, 1984.

Hengel, Martin. "*Mors turpissima crucis*: Die Kreuzigung in der antiken Welt und die 'Torheit' des 'Wortes vom Kreuz.'" In *Rechtfertigung: Festschrift für Ernst Käsemann zum 70. Geburtstag*, edited by Johannes Friedrich Wolfgang Pohlmann and Peter Stuhlmacher, 125–84. Tübingen: Mohr/Siebeck, 1976.

Jaffee, Martin S. "A Rabbinic Ontology of the Written and Spoken Word: On Discipleship, Transformative Knowledge, and the Living Texts of the Oral Torah." *JAAR* 65 (1997) 525–49.

Jobling, David, Tina Pippin, and Ronald Schleifer, editors. *The Postmodern Bible Reader.* Oxford: Blackwell, 2001.

King, Martin Luther, Jr. "A Comparison of the Conception of God in the Thinking of Paul Tillich and Henry Nelson Wieman." Ph.D. dissertation, Boston University, 1955.

———. "The Most Durable Power." *Christian Century* 74 (June 5, 1957) 10–11.

———. *Where Do We Go From Here: Chaos or Community?* New York: Harper & Row, 1967.

Koester, Helmut. "Jesus the Victim." *JBL* 111 (1992) 3–15.

Kugel, James L. *The Bible As It Was.* Cambridge, Mass.: Belknap, 1997.

———, and Rowan A. Greer. *Early Biblical Interpretation.* LEC 3. Philadelphia: Westminster, 1986.

Langbrandtner, Wolfgang. *Weltferner Gott oder Gott der Liebe: Die Ketzerstreit in der johanneischen Kirche.* BBET 6. Frankfurt: Lang, 1977.

Lightfoot, J. B. *Apostolic Fathers.* 2d ed. London: Macmillan, 1912.

Long, Charles. *Significations: Signs, Symbols, and Images in the Interpretation of Religion.* Philadelphia: Fortress Press, 1986.

MacRae, George W. "The Fourth Gospel and Religionsgeschichte." *CBQ* 32 (1970) 13–24.

Malina, Bruce J. "John: The Maverick Christian Group: The Evidence of Sociolinguistics." *BTB* 24 (1994) 167–82.

———, and Richard L. Rohrbaugh. *Social-Science Commentary on the Gospel of John.* Minneapolis: Fortress Press, 1998.

Marcus, Joel. "Rivers of Living Water from Jesus' Belly" (John 7:38)." *JBL* 117 (1998) 328–30.

Meeks, Wayne A. "Galilee and Judea in the Fourth Gospel." *JBL* 85 (1966) 159–69.

Miles, Jack. *God: A Biography.* New York: Knopf, 1995.

Moran, William L. "The Ancient Near Eastern Background of the Love of God in Deuteronomy." *CBQ* 25 (1963) 77–87.

Neyrey, Jerome H. "Despising the Shame of the Cross: Honor and Shame in the Johannine Passion Narrative." *Semeia* 69 (1994) 113–37.

Nickelsburg, George W. E. *Resurrection, Immortality, and Eternal Life in Intertestamental Judaism.* Harvard Theological Studies 26. Cambridge: Harvard Univ. Press, 1972.

Niebuhr, Reinhold. *An Interpretation of Christian Ethics.* New York: Meridian, 1958.

Nietzsche, Friedrich. *The Gay Science: With a Prelude in Rhymes and an Appendix of Songs.* Translated by Walter Kaufmann. New York: Random House, 1974.

Nouwen, Henri. *Lifesigns: Intimacy, Fecundity, and Ecstasy in Christian Perspective* (Garden City, N.Y.: Doubleday, 1986).

Nygren, Anders. *Agape and Eros: A Study of the Christian Idea of Love.* Translated by A. G. Herbert. New York: Macmillan, 1938.

Oded, Bustenay. "Observation on Methods of Assyrian Rule in Transjordania after the Palestinian Campaign of Tiglath-Pileser III." *Journal of Near Eastern Studies* 29 (1970) 177–86.

Perkins, Pheme. "Johannine Traditions in the *Ap. Jas.* (NHC I,2)." *JBL* 101 (1982) 403–14.

———. "*Koinōnia* in 1 John 1:3–7: The Social Context of Division in the Johannine Letters." *CBQ* 45 (1983) 631–41.

Piper, Otto A. "I John and the Didache of the Primitive Church." *JBL* 66 (1947) 437–51.

Prior, Michael. *The Bible and Colonialism: A Moral Critique.* Biblical Seminar 48. Sheffield: Sheffield Academic, 1997.

Ramsey, Paul. *Basic Christian Ethics.* Louisville: Westminster John Knox, 1993.

———. *Nine Modern Moralists.* Englewood Cliffs, N.J.: Prentice Hall, 1962.

Régamey, P.-R. *Poverty: An Essential Element in the Christian Life.* Translated by Rosemary Sheed. New York: Sheed and Ward, 1950.

Robinson, John A. T. "The Use of the Fourth Gospel for Christology Today." In *Christ and the Spirit in the New Testament*, edited by Barnabas Lindars and Stephen Smalley, 61–78. Cambridge: Cambridge Univ. Press, 1973.

Rubenstein, Jeffrey L. *The History of Sukkot in the Second Temple and Rabbinic Periods.* BJS 302. Atlanta: Scholars, 1995.

Schnackenburg, Rudolf. *The Gospel of John.* 3 vols. New York: Crossroad, 1968–82.

———. *The Johannine Epistles: Introduction and Commentary.* Translated by Reginald Fuller and Ilse Fuller. New York: Crossroad, 1992.

Smyth, Herbert Weir. *Greek Grammar.* Revised by Gordon M. Messing. Cambridge: Harvard Univ. Press, 1984.

Spicq, Ceslas. *Agape in the New Testament.* 3 vols. Translated by Marie Aquinas McNamara and Mary Honoria Richter. St. Louis: Herder, 1963–66. [*Agapè dans le Nouveau Testament: Analyse des Textes.* 3 vols. Paris: Gabalda, 1958.]

———. *Agapè: Prolégomènes à une étude de théologie néo-testamentaire.* Studia Hellenistica 10. Leiden: Brill, 1955.

Stählin, Otto, ed. *Clemens Alexandrinus.* Vol. 3. Berlin: Akademie, 1970.

Strack, H. L., and Günther Stemberger. *Introduction to the Talmud and Midrash.* 2d ed. Translated and edited by Markus Bockmuehl. Minneapolis: Fortress Press, 1996.

Strecker, Georg. *The Johannine Letters: A Commentary on 1, 2, and 3 John.* Translated by Linda M. Maloney. Edited by Harold W. Attridge. Hermeneia. Minneapolis: Fortress Press, 1996.

Tholuck, August, editor. *Ioannis Calvini in Novum Testamentum Commentarii.* Vol. 7. Berlin: Eichler, 1834.

Thompson, Thomas L. *Early History of the Israelite People from the Written and Archaeological Sources.* Studies in the History of the Ancient Near East 4. Leiden: Brill, 1992.

Tillich, Paul. *Dynamics of Faith.* New York: Harper, 1957.

Washington, James Melvin. *A Testament of Hope: The Essential Writings of Martin Luther King, Jr.* (San Francisco: Harper & Row, 1986).

Weems, Renita J. *Battered Love: Marriage, Sex, and Violence in the Hebrew Prophets.* OBT. Minneapolis: Fortress Press, 1995.

Weinfeld, Moshe. *The Promise of the Land: The Inheritance of the Land of Canaan by the Israelites*. Berkeley: Univ. of California Press, 1993.

Wescott, Brooke Foss. *Epistles of St. John*. London: Macmillan, 1883.

Wills, Garry. *Saint Augustine*. New York: Viking, 1999.

Wittgenstein, Ludwig. *Tractatus Logico-Philosophicus*. Translated by D. F. Pears and B. F. McGuiness. International Library of Philosophy and Scientific Method. New York: Humanities, 1963.

Younger, K. Lawson Jr. "The Deportation of the Israelites." *JBL* 117 (1998) 201–27.

Index of Ancient Sources